101 POEMS
for Children

CAROL ANN DUFFY
101 POEMS
for Children

A Laureate's Choice

Illustrated by Emily Gravett

MACMILLAN CHILDREN'S BOOKS

First published 2012 by Macmillan Children's Books
a division of Macmillan Publishers Limited
20 New Wharf Road, London N1 9RR
Basingstoke and Oxford
Associated companies throughout the world
www.panmacmillan.com

ISBN 978-1-4472-0516-6

1 3 5 7 9 8 6 4 2

A CIP catalogue record for this book is available from
the British Library.

Typeset by Ken de Silva
Printed and bound by CPI Group (UK) Ltd, Croydon CR0 4YY

For Ella with love from Mummy
ac i Morgan gyda chariad

CONTENTS

FOREWORD

Like most children, the first poems I encountered were nursery rhymes told to me by my mother, and the images they put into my head made these rhymes seem like magic spells – a dish ran away with a spoon; a cow jumped over the moon. I demanded to hear again and again about the crooked man who walked a crooked mile and the three blind mice. At school, I was lucky to have marvellous teachers who used a lot of poetry in the classroom. The first poem I learned by heart, when I was about ten, was 'The Song of Wandering Aengus' by W. B. Yeats. It's included in this anthology and is still one of my favourites – *'the silver apples of the moon, the golden apples of the sun.'* I was an avid reader as a child, and although I loved fiction (*Alice's Adventures in Wonderland* and Richmal Crompton's *William* books in particular) it was poetry whose luminous gravity kept me enthralled and smitten in its orbit. Poems, in so few words, create whole worlds, imaginary or real, and each poem seems to offer a different place from which to stand and look and listen. In this selection of 101 poems I've included some of those poems which I adored in my own childhood: 'The Lion and Albert', 'The Owl and the Pussycat', 'There Was an Old Lady Who Swallowed a Fly', 'Jabberwocky', 'There Was a Naughty Boy', and there are also poems here by some of our greatest children's poets, including Charles Causley and Ted Hughes.

In assembling this anthology I've tried to put together a poetry book that a child can live with for a long time – some poems here are lying in wait for future years. I hope that these poems will be shared, at least initially, between parent and child; that the child might want to learn one or two by heart; that the child who owns this book will grow with the poetry here and find poems that will stay with her or him forever.

Poetry, it was to turn out, gave me my life. As Gillian Clarke writes in her poem 'First Words':

> *The sea turns its pages, speaking in tongues.*
> *The stories are yours, and you are the story.*
> *And before you know it you'll know what comes*
> *from air and breath and off the page is all*
>
> *you'll want, like the sea's jewels in your hand,*
> *and the soft mutations of sea washing on sand.*

Poetry is generous. It is constantly offering us its music and imagery, expanding, if we will let it, into our hearts and minds from its modest space on the page. I hope, if you are a young reader who is given this book, that you'll find many poems here – funny, sad, mysterious or familiar – that will remain with you as you grow.

Carol Ann Duffy

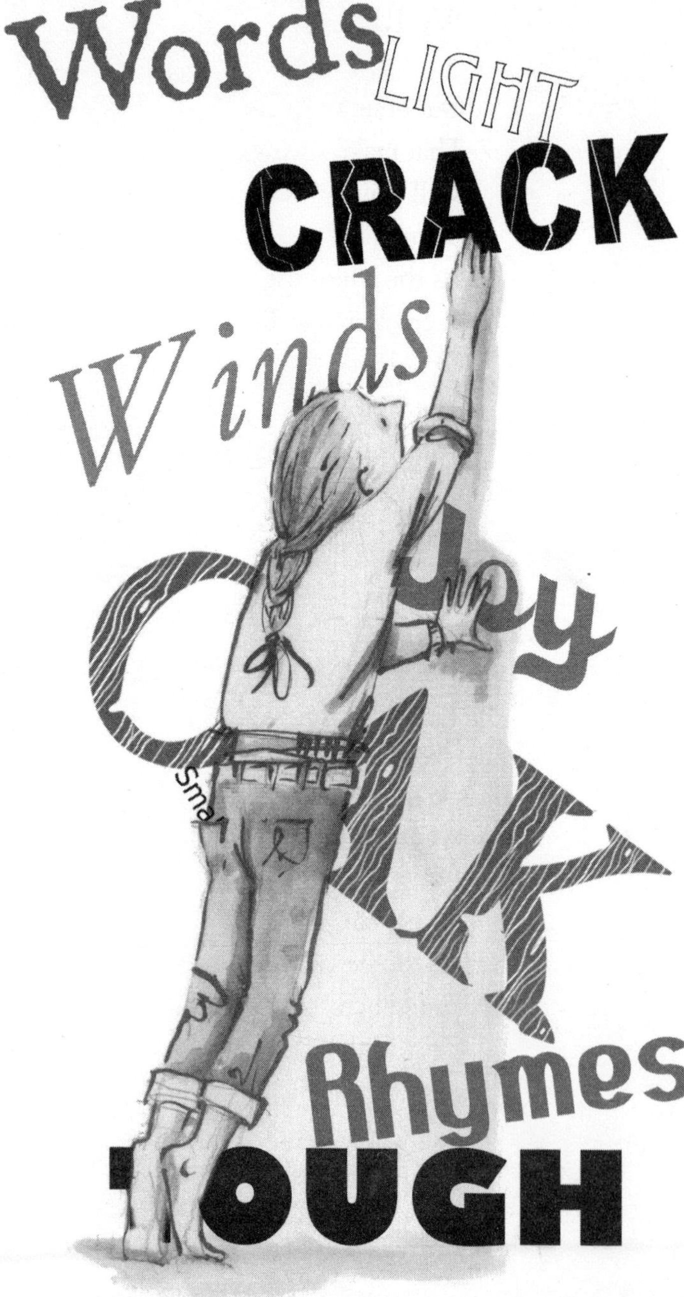
Words
LIGHT
CRACK
Winds
Rhymes

WORDS

Out of us all
That make rhymes,
Will you choose
Sometimes –
As the winds use
A crack in a wall
Or a drain,
Their joy or their pain
To whistle through –
Choose me,
You English words?

I know you:
You are light as dreams,
Tough as oak,
Precious as gold,
As poppies and corn,
Or an old cloak;
Sweet as our birds
To the ear,
As the burnet rose
In the heat
Of Midsummer:

Strange as the races
Of dead and unborn:
Strange and sweet
Equally,
And familiar,
To the eye,
As the dearest faces
That a man knows,
And as lost homes are:
But though older far
Than oldest yew –
As our hills are, old –
Worn new
Again and again:
Young as our streams
After rain:
And as dear
As the earth which you prove
That we love.

Make me content
With some sweetness
From Wales,
Whose nightingales
Have no wings –
From Wiltshire and Kent
And Herefordshire,
And the villages there –
From the names, and the things
No less.
Let me sometimes dance
With you,
Or climb,
Or stand perchance
In ecstasy,
Fixed and free
In a rhyme,
As poets do.

EDWARD THOMAS

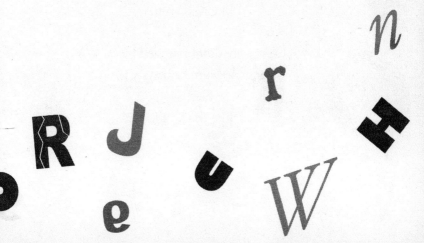

STUFFERATION

Lovers lie around in it
Broken glass is found in it
Grass
I like that stuff

Tuna fish get trapped in it
Legs come wrapped in it
Nylon
I like that stuff

Eskimos and tramps chew it
Madame Tussaud gave status to it
Wax
I like that stuff

Elephants get sprayed with it
Scotch is made with it
Water
I like that stuff

Clergy are dumbfounded by it
Bones are surrounded by it
Flesh
I like that stuff

Harps are strung with it
Mattresses are sprung with it
Wire
I like that stuff

Carpenters make cots of it
Undertakers use lots of it
Wood
I like that stuff

Dirty cigarettes are lit by it
Pensioners get happy when they sit by it
Fire
I like that stuff

Johnny Dankworth's alto is made of it, most of it*
Scoubidou is composed of it**
Plastic
I like that stuff

*Jazz musician John Dankworth used to play a plastic saxophone.
**Scoubidou was a fistful of kind of multi-coloured pieces of plastic which were a
playground craze in the 1950s. It was a sad sort of toy, nothing like the exciting
Hula Hoop of the same period.

Elvis kept it in his left-hand pocket
Little Richard made it zoom like a rocket
Rock 'n' Roll
Ooh my soul
I like that stuff

Apemen take it to make them hairier
I ate a ton of it in Bulgaria
Yogurt
I like that stuff

Man-made fibres and raw materials
Old rolled gold and breakfast cereals
Platinum linoleum
I like that stuff

Skin on my hands
Hair on my head
Toenails on my feet
And linen on the bed

Well I like that stuff
Yes I like that stuff
The earth
Is made of earth
And I like that stuff

ADRIAN MITCHELL

A BIRD CAME DOWN

A bird came down the walk:
He did not know I saw;
He bit an angle-worm in halves
And ate the fellow, raw.

And then he drank a dew
From a convenient grass,
And then hopped sidewise to the wall
To let a beetle pass.

He glanced with rapid eyes
That hurried all abroad,—
They looked like frightened beads, I thought;
He stirred his velvet head

Like one in danger; cautious,
I offered him a crumb,
And he unrolled his feathers
And rowed him softer home

Than oars divide the ocean,
Too silver for a seam,
Or butterflies, off banks of noon,
Leap, splashless, as they swim.

EMILY DICKINSON

BLACKBERRY EATING

I love to go out in late September
among the fat, overripe, icy, black blackberries
to eat blackberries for breakfast,
the stalks very prickly, a penalty .
they earn for knowing the black art
of blackberry making; and as I stand among them
lifting the stalks to my mouth, the ripest berries
fall almost unbidden to my tongue,
as words sometimes do, certain peculiar words
like *strengths* or *squinched* or *broughamed*,
many-lettered, one-syllabled lumps,
which I squeeze, squinch open, and splurge well
in the silent, startled, icy, black language
of blackberry eating in late September.

GALWAY KINNELL

9

THIS IS JUST TO SAY

I have eaten
the plums
that were in
the icebox

and which
you were probably
saving
for breakfast

Forgive me
they were delicious
so sweet
and so cold

WILLIAM CARLOS WILLIAMS

THE APPLE'S SONG

Tap me with your finger,
rub me with your sleeve,
hold me, sniff me, peel me
curling round and round
till I burst out white and cold
from my tight red coat
and tingle in your palm
as if I'd melt and breathe
a living pomander
waiting for the minute
of joy when you lift me
to your mouth and crush me
and in taste and fragrance
I race through your head
in my dizzy dissolve.

I sit in the bowl
in my cool corner
and watch you as you pass
smoothing your apron.
Are you thirsty yet?
My eyes are shining.

EDWIN MORGAN

HOW TO CUT A POMEGRANATE

'Never,' said my father.
'Never cut a pomegranate
through the heart. It will weep blood.
Treat it delicately, with respect.

Just slit the upper skin across four quarters.
This is a magic fruit,
so when you split it open, be prepared
for the jewels of the world to tumble out,
more precious than garnets,
more lustrous than rubies,
lit as if from inside.
Each jewel contains a living seed.
Separate one crystal.
Hold it up to catch the light.
Inside is a whole universe.
No common jewel can give you this.'

Afterwards, I tried to make necklaces
of pomegranate seeds.
The juice spurted out, bright crimson,
and stained my fingers, then my mouth.

I didn't mind. The juice tasted of gardens
I had never seen, voluptuous
with myrtle, lemon, jasmine,
and alive with parrots' wings.

The pomegranate reminded me
that somewhere I had another home.

IMTIAZ DHARKER

FIRST WORDS

The alphabet of a house – air,
breath, the creak of the stair.
Downstairs the grown-ups' hullabaloo,
or their hush as you fall asleep.

You're learning the language: the steel slab
of a syllable dropped at the docks; the two-beat word
of the Breaksea lightship; the golden sentence
of a train crossing the viaduct.

Later, at Fforest, all the words are new.
You are your grandmother's Cariad, not Darling.
Tide and current are *llanw, lli*.
The waves repeat their *ll-ll-ll* on sand.

Over the sea the starlings come in paragraphs.
She tells you a tale of a girl and a bird,
reading it off the tide in lines of longhand
that scatter to bits on the shore.

The sea turns its pages, speaking in tongues.
The stories are yours, and you are the story.
And before you know it you'll know what comes
from air and breath and off the page is all

you'll want, like the sea's jewels in your hand,
and the soft mutations of sea washing on sand.

GILLIAN CLARKE

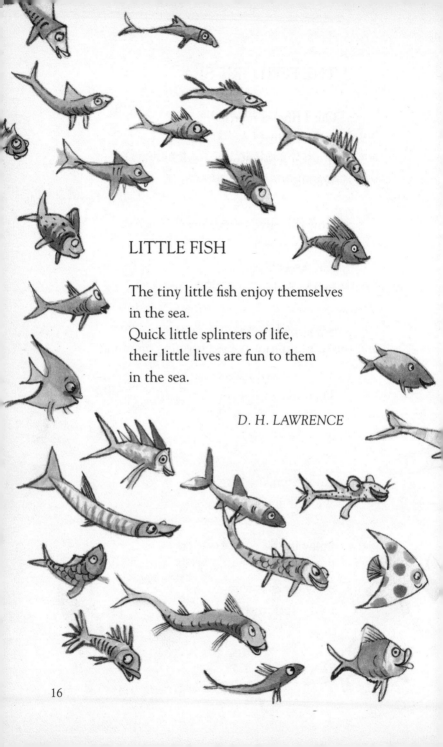

LITTLE FISH

The tiny little fish enjoy themselves
in the sea.
Quick little splinters of life,
their little lives are fun to them
in the sea.

D. H. LAWRENCE

THE FORLORN SEA

Our Princess married
A fairy King,
It was a sensational
Wedding.

Now they live in a palace
Of porphyry,
Far, far away,
By the forlorn sea.

Sometimes people visit them,
Last week they invited me;
That is how I can tell you
They live by a forlorn sea.

(They said: Here's a magic carpet,
Come on this,
And when you arrive
We will give you a big kiss.)

I play in the palace garden,
I climb the sycamore tree,
Sometimes I swim
In the forlorn sea.

The King and the Princess are shadowy,
Yet beautiful,
They are waited on by white cats,
Who are dutiful.

It is like a dream
When they kiss and cuddle me,
But I like it, I like it,
I do not wish to break free.

So I eat all they give me
Because I have read
If you eat fairy food
You will never wake up in your own bed,

But will go on living,
As has happened to me,
Far, far away
By a forlorn sea.

STEVIE SMITH

THE EMERGENSEA

The octopus awoke one morning and wondered what
    rhyme it was.
Looking at his alarm-clocktopus
he saw that it had stopped
and it was time to stop having a rest
and get himself dressed.
On every octofoot
he put
an octosocktopus
but in his hurry, one foot got put
not into an octosocktopus
but into an electric outlet
and the octopus got a nasty electric shocktopus
and had to call the octodoctopus
who couldn't get in
to give any help or medicine
because the door was loctopus.
The octopus couldn't move, being in a state of
    octoshocktopus
so the octodoctopus bashed the door
to the floor
and the cure was as simple as could be:
a nice refreshing cup of
seawater.

JOHN HEGLEY

FISHBONES DREAMING

Fishbones lay in the smelly bin.
He was a head, a backbone and a tail.
Soon the cats would be in for him.
He didn't like to be this way.
He shut his eyes and dreamed back.
Back to when he was fat, and hot on a plate.
Beside green beans, with lemon juice
squeezed on him. And a man with a knife
and fork raised, about to eat him.
He didn't like to be this way.
He shut his eyes and dreamed back.
Back to when he was frozen in the freezer.
With lamb cutlets and minced beef and prawns.
Three month he was in there.
He didn't like to be this way.

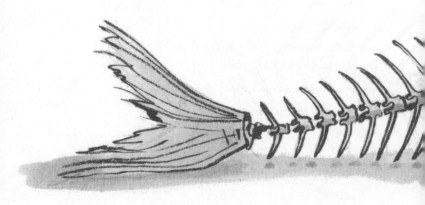

He shut his eyes and dreamed back.
Back to when he was squirming in a net,
with thousands of other fish, on the deck
of a boat. And the rain falling
Wasn't wet enough to breathe in.
He didn't like to be this way.
He shut his eyes and dreamed back.
Back to when he was darting through the sea,
past crabs and jellyfish, and others
likes himself. Or surfacing to jump for flies
And feel the sun on his face.
He liked to be this way.
He dreamed hard to try and stay there.

MATTHEW SWEENEY

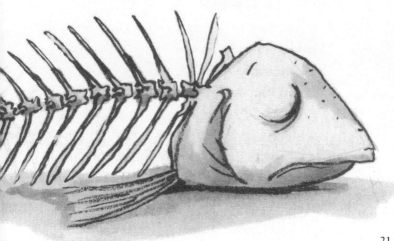

TEN THINGS FOUND IN A SHIPWRECKED SAILOR'S POCKET

A litre of sea.
An unhappy jellyfish.
A small piece of a lifeboat.
A pencil wrapped around with seaweed.
A soaking feather.
The first page of a book called *Swimming Is Easy*.
A folded chart showing dangerous rocks.
A photograph of a little girl in a red dress.
A gold coin.
A letter from a mermaid.

IAN McMILLAN

BEACHCOMBER

Monday I found a boot –
Rust and salt leather,
I gave it back to the sea, to dance in.

Tuesday a spar of timber worth thirty bob.
Next winter
It will be a chair, a coffin, a bed.

Wednesday a half can of Swedish spirits.
I tilted my head.
The shore was cold with mermaids and angels.

Thursday I got nothing, seaweed,
A whale bone,
Wet feet and a bad cough.

Friday I held a seaman's skull,
Sand spilling from it
The way time is told on kirkyard stones.

Saturday a barrel of sodden oranges.
A Spanish ship
Was wrecked last month at The Kame.

Sunday, for fear of the elders,
I smoke on the stone.
What's heaven? A sea chest with a thousand
    gold coins.

GEORGE MACKAY BROWN

THE DRAGONFLY

There was once a terrible monster
lived in a pond, deep under the water.

Brown as mud he was, in the mud he hid,
among murk of reed-roots, sodden twigs,
with his long hungry belly,
six legs for creeping,
eyes like headlights
awake or sleeping:
but he was not big.

A tiddler came to sneer and jeer
and flaunt his flashing tail –
Ugly old stick-in-the-mud,
couldn't catch a snai-l!
I'm not scared –
when, like a shot,
two pincers nab him, and he's got!

For the monster's jaw hides a clawed stalk
like the arm of a robot, a dinner fork,
that's tucked away cunningly till the last minute –
shoots out – and back with a victim in it!

Days, weeks, months, two years and beyond,
fear of the monster beset the pond;
he lurked, grabbed, grappled, gobbled and grew,
ambushing always somewhere new –

Who saw him last? Does anyone know?
Don't go near the mud! But I must go!
Keep well away from the rushes! But how?
Has anyone seen my sister? Not for a week now –
she's been eaten
for certain!

And then one day, it was June, they all saw him,
he was coming slowly up out of the mud,
they stopped swimming. No one dared
approach, attack. They kept back.

Up a tall reed they saw him climbing
higher and higher, until
he broke the surface, climbing still.

There he stopped, in the wind and the setting sun.
We're safe at last! they cried. *He's gone!*

What became of the monster? Was he ill, was he sad?
Was nobody sorry? Had he crept off to die? Was he mad?

Not one of them saw how, suddenly,
as if an invisible knife had touched his back,
he has split, split completely –
his head split like a lid!

The cage is open. Slowly he comes through,
an emperor, with great eyes burning blue.

He rests then, veils of silver a cloak for him.
Night and the little stars travel the black pond.
And now, first light of the day,
his shining cloak wide wings, a flash, a whirr,
a jewelled helicopter,
he's away!

O fully he had served his time,
shunned and unlovely in the drab slime,
for freedom at the end – for the sky –
dazzling hunter, Dragonfly!

LIBBY HOUSTON

CATERPILLAR

He stands on the suckers under his tail,
stretches forward and puts down
his six legs. Then he brings up
the sucker under his tail, making
a beautiful loop.

That's his way of walking. He makes
a row of upside-down U's
along the rib of a leaf. He is as green
as it.

The ways of walking! – horse, camel,
snail, me, crab, rabbit –
all inventing a way of journeying
till they become like the green caterpillar
that now stands on his tail
on the very tip of the leaf and sways, sways
like a tiny charmed snake,
groping in empty space for a foothold
where none is, where there is no
foothold at all.

NORMAN MacCAIG

THE DREAM OF THE
CABBAGE CATERPILLARS

There was no magic spell:
all of us, sleeping,
dreamed the same dream – a dream
that's ours for the keeping.

In sunbeam or dripping rain,
sister by brother
we once roamed with glee
the leaves that our mother

laid us and left us on,
browsing our fill
of green cabbage, fresh cabbage,
thick cabbage, until

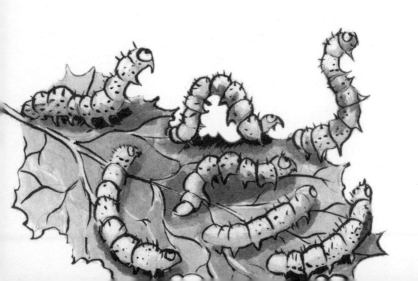

in the hammocks we hung
from the garden wall
came sleep, and the dream
that changed us all –

we had left our soft bodies,
the munching, the crawling,
to skim through the clear air
like white petals falling!

Just so, so we woke –
so to skip high as towers,
and dip now to sweet fuel
from trembling bright flowers.

LIBBY HOUSTON

TOAD

Stop looking like a purse. How could a purse
squeeze under the rickety door and sit,
full of satisfaction, in a man's house?

You clamber towards me on your four corners –
right hand, left foot, left hand, right foot.

I love you for being a toad,
for crawling like a Japanese wrestler,
and for not being frightened.

I put you in my purse hand, not shutting it,
and set you down outside directly under
every star.

A jewel in your head? Toad,
you've put one in mine,
a tiny radiance in a dark place.

NORMAN MacCAIG

THE FOX AND THE GIRL

Once her father came home with a fox cub
in his coat pocket. Lost in the city,
shivering in rubbish outside the pub,
the colour of conkers and as pretty

as a puppy, its teeth like needles.
It hissed in her arms, but she wheedled
to keep it. When it bit her she cried
for her bloody hand, and she cried

when he said, 'Mae'n wyllt. It's a wild
animal, not a pet for a child.'
She could feel its life, its warm fur,
its quick heart beating against her.

and she hurt for its animal mystery,
for the vanishing story of a girl
and a fox lost for words
in the secret forest.

GILLIAN CLARKE

F FOR FOX

The fox fled over the fields away from the farm
and the furious farmer.
                              His fur was freaked.
His foxy face was frantic as he flew. A few feathers
fluttered out of his mouth.
                              The fox
had broken his fast with a feast of fowl!
The farmer had threatened to flay the fur
from his frame.
                              The frightened fox flung himself
at a fence.

                The fox found himself in a fairground,
with a Ferris wheel, flashing lights, fruit machines, fish
in plastic bags.
                              Furtively, he foraged for food –
fragments of candyfloss, French fries –
but a fella folding fivers into his fist
flicked a fiery fag at the fox and the fox foxed off.

Further and further fled the fox, through Forfar, Fife, Falkirk,
forests, fields, Fleetwood, Fazakerley, thunder and fog,
famished and fearful;
                                   forcing his furry features
into family bins, filching thrown-away food.
Thief fox, friendless fox, thin fox. Finally
he came at first light to a faraway farm . . .

where the fox fed himself full
till his face was fat
and forlorn feathers floated away on the frosty air.

CAROL ANN DUFFY

HORRIBLE SONG

The Crow is a wicked creature
    Crooked in every feature.
Beware, beware of the Crow!
When the bombs burst, he laughs, he shouts;
When guns go off, he roundabouts;
When the limbs start to fly and the blood starts to flow
    Ho Ho Ho
    He sings the Song of the Crow.

The Crow is a sudden creature
    Thievish in every feature.
Beware, beware of the Crow!
When the sweating farmers sleep
He levers the jewels from the heads of their sheep.
Die in a ditch, your own will go,
    Ho Ho Ho
    While he sings the Song of the Crow.

The Crow is a subtle creature
    Cunning in every feature.
Beware, beware of the Crow!
When sick folk tremble on their cots
He sucks their souls through the chimney pots,
They're dead and gone before they know,
    Ho Ho Ho
    And he sings the Song of the Crow.

The crow is a lusty creature
    Gleeful in every feature.
Beware, beware of the Crow!
If he can't get your liver, he'll find an old rat
Or highway hedgehog hammered flat,
Any old rubbish to make him grow,
    Ho Ho Ho
    While he sings the Song of the Crow.

The Crow is a hardy creature
    Fireproof in every feature.
Beware, beware of the Crow!
When Mankind's blasted to kingdom come
The Crow will dance and hop and drum
And into an old thigh bone he'll blow
    Ho Ho Ho
    Singing the Song of the Crow.

TED HUGHES

A CROW AND A SCARECROW

A crow and a scarecrow fell in love
out in the fields.
The scarecrow's heart was a stuffed leather glove
but his love was real.
The crow perched on the stick of a wrist
and opened her beak:
Scarecrow, I love you madly, deeply.
Speak.

Crow, rasped the Scarecrow, *hear these words*
from my straw throat.
I love you too
from my boot to my hat
by way of my old tweed coat.
Croak.
The crow crowed back,
Scarecrow, let me take you away
to live in a tall tree.
I'll be a true crow wife to you
if you'll marry me.

The Scarecrow considered.
Crow, tell me how
a groom with a broomstick spine
can take a bride.
I know you believe in the love
in these button eyes
but I'm straw inside
and straw can't fly.

The crow pecked at his heart
with her beak
then flapped away,
and back and forth she flew to him
all day, all day,
until she pulled one last straw
from his tattered vest
and soared across the sun with it
to her new nest.

And there she slept, high in her tree,
winged, in a bed of love.
Night fell.
The slow moon rose
over a meadow,
a heap of clothes,
two boots,
an empty glove.

CAROL ANN DUFFY

THE SLEEP OF BIRDS

We cannot hear the birds sleeping
Under the trees, under the flowers, under the eyes of our
    watching
And the rustling over of sheets of our unsleeping
Or our final whispers of loving.
How enviable this solemn silence of theirs
Like the quiet of monks tired with their singing hours
And dreaming about the next.
Birds are remote as stars by being silent
And will flash out like stars at their punctual dawn
As the stars are snuffed by the sun.

Does this quiet sleep of birds hide dreams, hide nightmares?
Does the lash of wind and the failing wing and the falling
Out of the air enter their sleep? Let us listen,
Open the window and listen
For a cry of a nightmare to underline the night.
There is no cry, there is only
The one feathered life who's not awake and does not sing
But hoots and holds his own, his own now being
A lordly and humorous comment upon the darkness,
A quiet joke at the changing demands of the moon.

ELIZABETH JENNINGS

ST FRANCIS AND THE BIRDS

When Francis preached love to the birds
They listened, fluttered, throttled up
Into the blue like a flock of words

Released for fun from his holy lips.
Then wheeled back, whirred about his head,
Pirouetted on brothers' capes.

Danced on the wing, for sheer joy played
And sang, like images took flight.
Which was the best poem Francis made,

His argument true, his tone light.

SEAMUS HEANEY

THE BLACKBIRD

In the far corner
close by the swings
every morning
a blackbird sings.

His bill's so yellow
his coat's so black
that he makes a fellow
whistle back.

Ann my daughter
thinks that he
sings for us two
especially.

HUMBERT WOLFE

HYENA

I am waiting for you.
I have been travelling all morning through the bush
and not eaten.
I am lying at the edge of the bush
on a dusty path that leads from the burnt-out kraal.
I am panting, it is midday, I found no water-hole.
I am very fierce without food and although my eyes
are screwed to slits against the sun
you must believe I am prepared to spring.

What do you think of me?
I have a rough coat like Africa.
I am crafty with dark spots
like the bush-tufted plains of Africa.
I sprawl as a shaggy bundle of gathered energy
like Africa sprawling in its waters.
I trot, I lope, I slaver, I am a ranger.
I hunch my shoulders. I eat the dead.

Do you like my song?
When the moon pours hard and cold on the veldt
I sing, and I am the slave of darkness.
Over the stone walls and the mud walls and the ruined places
and the owls, the moonlight falls.
I sniff a broken drum. I bristle. My pelt is silver.
I howl my song to the moon – up it goes.
Would you meet me there in the waste places?

It is said I am a good match
for a dead lion. I put my muzzle
at his golden flanks, and tear. He
is my golden supper, but my tastes are easy.
I have a crowd of fangs, and I use them.
Oh and my tongue – do you like me
When it comes lolling out over my jaw
very long, and I am laughing?
I am not laughing.
But I am not snarling either, only
panting in the sun, showing you
what I grip
carrion with.

I am waiting
for the foot to slide,
for the heart to seize,
for the leaping sinews to go slack,
for the fight to the death to be fought to the death,
for a glazing eye and the rumour of blood.
I am crouching in my dry shadows
till you are ready for me.
My place is to pick you clean
and leave your bones to the wind.

EDWIN MORGAN

THE LION AND ALBERT

There's a famous seaside place called Blackpool,
    That's noted for fresh air and fun,
And Mr and Mrs Ramsbottom
    Went there with young Albert, their son.

A grand little lad was young Albert,
    All dressed in his best; quite a swell
With a stick with an 'orse's 'ead 'andle,
    The finest that Woolworth's could sell.

They didn't think much to the Ocean:
    The waves, they was fiddlin' and small,
There was no wrecks and nobody drownded,
    Fact, nothing to laugh at at all.

So, seeking for further amusement,
    They paid and went into the Zoo,
Where they'd Lions and Tigers and Camels,
    And old ale and sandwiches too.

There were one great big Lion called Wallace;
    His nose were all covered with scars –
He lay in a somnolent posture,
    With the side of his face on the bars.

Now Albert had heard about Lions,
    How they was ferocious and wild –
To see Wallace lying so peaceful,
    Well, it didn't seem right to the child.

So straightway the brave little feller,
    Not showing a morsel of fear,
Took his stick with its 'orse's 'ead 'andle
    . . . And pushed it in Wallace's ear.

You could see that the Lion didn't like it,
    For giving a kind of a roll,
He pulled Albert inside the cage with 'im,
    And swallowed the little lad 'ole.

Then Pa, who had seen the occurrence,
    And didn't know what to do next,
Said 'Mother! Yon Lion's 'et Albert',
    And Mother said 'Well I am vexed!'

Then Mr and Mrs Ramsbottom –
    Quite rightly, when all's said and done –
Complained to the Animal Keeper,
    That the Lion had eaten their son.

The keeper was quite nice about it;
    He said 'What a nasty mishap.
Are you sure that it's your boy he's eaten?'
    Pa said 'Am I sure? There's his cap!'

The manager had to be sent for.
    He came and he said 'What's to do?'
Pa said 'Yon Lion's 'et Albert,
    And 'im in his Sunday clothes too.'

Then Mother said 'Right's right, young feller;
    I think it's a shame and a sin,
For a lion to go and eat Albert,
    And after we've paid to come in.'

The manager wanted no trouble,
　　He took out his purse right away,
Saying 'How much to settle the matter?'
　　And Pa said 'What do you usually pay?'

But Mother had turned a bit awkward
　　When she thought where her Albert had gone.
She said 'No! someone's got to be summonsed' –
　　So that was decided upon.

Then off they went to the P'lice Station,
　　In front of the Magistrate chap;
They told 'im what happened to Albert,
　　And proved it by showing his cap.

The Magistrate gave his opinion
　　That no one was really to blame
And he said that he hoped the Ramsbottoms
　　Would have further sons to their name.

At that Mother got proper blazing,
　　'And thank you, sir, kindly,' said she.
'What waste all our lives raising children
　　To feed ruddy Lions? Not me!'

MARRIOTT EDGAR

GOOD MORNING, MR CROCO-DOCO-DILE

Good Morning, Mr Croco-doco-dile,
And how are you today?
I like to see your croco-smoco-smile,
In your croco-woco-way.

From the tip of your beautiful croco-toco-tail,
To your croco-hoco-head,
You seem to me so croco-stoco-still,
As if you are coco-doco-dead.

Perhaps if I touch your croco-cloco-claw,
Or your croco-snoco-snout,
Or get up to your croco-joco-jaw,
I shall very soon find out.

But suddenly I croco-soco-see,
In your croco-oco-eye,
A curious kind of croco-gloco-gleam,
So I just don't think I'll try.

Forgive me, Mr Croco-doco-dile,
But it's time I was away,
Let's talk a little croco-woco-while,
Another croco-doco-day.

CHARLES CAUSLEY

TO A SQUIRREL AT KYLE-NA-NO

Come play with me;
Why should you run
Through the shaking tree
As though I'd a gun
To strike you dead?
When all I would do
Is to scratch your head
And let you go.

W. B. YEATS

FOR I WILL CONSIDER MY CAT JEOFFRY

For I will consider my Cat Jeoffry.

For he is the servant of the Living God, duly and daily serving him.

For at the first glance of the glory of God in the East he worships in his way.

For this is done by wreathing his body seven times round with elegant quickness.

For then he leaps up to catch the musk, which is the blessing of God upon his prayer.

For he rolls upon prank to work it in.

For having done duty and received blessing he begins to consider himself.

For this he performs in ten degrees.

For first he looks upon his forepaws to see if they are clean.

For secondly he kicks up behind to clear away there.

For thirdly he works it upon stretch with the forepaws
    extended.

For fourthly he sharpens his paws by wood.

For fifthly he washes himself.

For sixthly he rolls upon wash.

For seventhly he fleas himself, that he may not be
    interrupted upon the beat.

For eighthly he rubs himself against a post.

For ninthly he looks up for his instructions.

For tenthly he goes in quest of food.

For having considered God and himself he will consider his
    neighbour.

For if he meets another cat he will kiss her in kindness.

For when he takes his prey he plays with it to give it a chance.

For one mouse in seven escapes by his dallying.

For when his day's work is done his business more properly begins.

For he keeps the Lord's watch in the night against the adversary.

For he counteracts the powers of darkness by his electrical skin and glaring eyes.

For he counteracts the Devil, who is death, by brisking about the life.

For in his morning orisons he loves the sun and the sun loves him.

For he is of the tribe of Tiger.

For the Cherub Cat is a term of the Angel Tiger.

For he has the subtlety and hissing of a serpent, which in goodness he suppresses.

For he will not do destruction if he is well fed, neither will he spit without provocation.

For he purrs in thankfulness when God tells him he's a good Cat.

For he is an instrument for the children to learn benevolence upon.

For every house is incomplete without him, and a blessing is lacking in the spirit.

For the Lord commanded Moses concerning the cats at the departure of the Children of Israel
	from Egypt.

For every family had one Cat at least in the bag.

For the English Cats are the best in Europe.

For he is the cleanest in the use of his forepaws of any quadruped.

For the dexterity of his defence is an instance of the love of God to him exceedingly.

For he is the quickest to his mark of any creature.

For he is tenacious of his point.

For he is a mixture of gravity and waggery.

For he knows that God is his Saviour.

For there is nothing sweeter than his peace when at rest.

For there is nothing brisker than his life when in motion.

For he is of the Lord's poor, and so indeed is he called by
benevolence perpetually—Poor Jeoffry!
poor Jeoffry! the rat has bit thy throat.

For I bless the name of the Lord Jesus that Jeoffry is better.

For the divine spirit comes about his body to sustain it in
complete cat.

For his tongue is exceeding pure so that it has in purity what
it wants in music.

For he is docile and can learn certain things.

For he can sit up with gravity, which is patience upon
approbation.

For he can fetch and carry, which is patience in employment.

For he can jump over a stick, which is patience upon proof
positive.

For he can spraggle upon waggle at the word of command.

For he can jump from an eminence into his master's bosom.

For he can catch the cork and toss it again.

For he is hated by the hypocrite and miser.

For the former is afraid of detection.

For the latter refuses the charge.

For he camels his back to bear the first notion of business.

For he is good to think on, if a man would express himself
    neatly.

For he made a great figure in Egypt for his signal services.

For he killed the Icneumon rat, very pernicious by land.

For his ears are so acute that they sting again.

For from this proceeds the passing quickness of his attention.

For by stroking of him I have found out electricity.

For I perceived God's light about him both wax and fire.

For the electrical fire is the spiritual substance which God
    sends from heaven to sustain the
        bodies both of man and beast.

For God has blessed him in the variety of his movements.

For, though he cannot fly, he is an excellent clamberer.

For his motions upon the face of the earth are more than any
    other quadruped.

For he can tread to all the measures upon the music.

For he can swim for life.

For he can creep.

CHRISTOPHER SMART

56

THE OWL AND THE PUSSYCAT

1.
The Owl and the Pussycat went to sea
    In a beautiful pea-green boat,
They took some honey, and plenty of money,
    Wrapped up in a five-pound note.
The Owl looked up to the stars above,
    And sang to a small guitar,
'O lovely Pussy! O Pussy, my love,
    What a beautiful Pussy you are,
        You are,
        You are!
What a beautiful Pussy you are!'

2.

Pussy said to the Owl, 'You elegant fowl!
    How charmingly sweet you sing!
O let us be married! too long we have tarried:
    But what shall we do for a ring?'
They sailed away, for a year and a day,
    To the land where the Bong-Tree grows
And there in a wood a Piggy-wig stood
    With a ring at the end of his nose,
        His nose,
        His nose,
With a ring at the end of his nose.

3.

'Dear Pig, are you willing to sell for one shilling
    Your ring?' Said the Piggy, 'I will.'
So they took it away, and were married next day
    By the Turkey who lives on the hill.
They dined on mince, and slices of quince,
    Which they ate with a runcible spoon;
And hand in hand, on the edge of the sand,
    They danced by the light of the moon,
       The moon,
       The moon,
They danced by the light of the moon.

EDWARD LEAR

TO A MOUSE

Wee, sleekit, cowran, tim'rous beastie,
  O, what a panic's in thy breastie!
Thou need na start awa sae hasty,
      Wi' bickering brattle!
I wad be laith to rin an' chase thee,
      Wi' murd'ring pattle!

I'm truly sorry Man's dominion
Has broken Nature's social union,
    An' justifies that ill opinion,
      Which makes thee startle,
At me, thy poor, earth-born companion,
      An' fellow-mortal!

I doubt na, whyles, but thou may thieve;
What then? poor beastie, thou maun live!
A daimen-icker in a thrave 'S a sma' request:
    I'll get a blessin wi' the lave,
      An' never miss't!

Thy wee-bit housie, too, in ruin!
It's silly wa's the win's are strewin!
An' naething, now, to big a new ane,
      O' foggage green!
An' bleak December's winds ensuin,
      Baith snell an' keen!

Thou saw the fields laid bare an' wast,
    An' weary Winter comin fast,
    An' cozie here, beneath the blast,

Thou thought to dwell,
Till crash! the cruel coulter past
Out thro' thy cell.
That wee-bit heap o' leaves an' stibble,
Has cost thee monie a weary nibble!
Now thou's turn'd out, for a' thy trouble,
But house or hald.
To thole the Winter's sleety dribble,
An' cranreuch cauld!
But Mousie, thou are no thy-lane,
In proving foresight may be vain:
The best-laid schemes o' Mice an' Men,
Gang aft agley,
An' lea'e us nought but grief an' pain,
For promis'd joy!
Still, thou art blest, compar'd wi' me!
The present only toucheth thee:
But Och! I backward cast my e'e,
On prospects drear!
An' forward, tho' I canna see,
I guess an' fear!

ROBERT BURNS

RAT-PSALM

Sing the hole's plume, the rafter's cockade
Who melts from the eye-corner, the soft squealer
Pointed at both ends, who chews through lead

Sing the scholarly meek face
Of the penniless Rat
Who studies all night
To inherit the house

Sing the riffraff of the roof-space, who dance till dawn
Sluts in silk, sharpers with sleek moustaches
Dancing the cog-roll, the belly-bounce, the trundle

Sing the tireless hands
Of the hardworking Rat
Who demolishes the crust, and does not fail
To sign the spilt flour.

The Rat the Rat the Ratatatat
The house's poltergeist, shaped like a shuttle
Who longs to join the family

Sing his bright face, cross-eyed with eagerness
His pin fingers, that seem too small for the job
Sing his split nose, that looks so sore
O sing his fearless ears, the listener in the wall
Let him jump on your head, let him cling there
Save him from sticks and stones

Sing the Rat so poor he thrives on poison
Who has nothing to give to the trap, though it gapes for a year
Except his children
Who prays only to the ferret
'Forget me' and to the terrier
'In every million of me, spare two'

Who stuffs his velvet purse, in hurry and fear
With the memory of the fork,
The reflections of the spoons, the hope of the knives
Who woos his wife with caperings, who thinks deep

Who is the slave of two fangs

O sing
The long-tailed grey worry of the night hours
Who always watches and waits
Like a wart on the nose
Even while you snore

O sing
Little Jesus in the wilderness
Carrying the sins of the house
Into every dish, the hated one

O sing
Scupper-tyke, whip-lobber
Smutty-guts, pot-goblin
Garret-whacker, rick-lark
Sump-swab, cupboard-adder
Bobby-robin, knacker-knocker
Sneak-nicker, sprinty-dinty
Pintle-bum

TED HUGHES

RAT IT UP

C'mon everybody
Slap some grease on those paws
Get some yellow on your teeth
And, uh, sharpen up your claws

There's a whole lot of sausage
We're gonna swallow down
We're gonna jump out the sewers
And rock this town

Cos we're ratting it up
Yes, we're ratting it up
Well, we're ratting it up
For a ratting good time tonight

Ain't got no compass
You don't need no map
Just follow your snout
Hey, watch out for that trap!

You can take out a poodle
You can beat up a cat
But if you can't lick a ferret
You ain't no kind of rat

Cos we're ratting it up
Yes, we're ratting it up
Well, we're ratting it up
For a ratting good time tonight

Now you can sneak in the henhouse
Roll out the eggs
But if the farmer comes running
Bite his hairy legs

Check the cheese for poison
Before you eat
Or you'll wind up being served up
As ratburger meat

Cos we're ratting it up
Yes, we're ratting it up
Well, we're ratting it up
For a ratting good time tonight

This rat was born to rock
This rat was born to roll
I don't give a monkeys
Bout your pest control

So push off pussycat
Push off, pup,
We're the rocking rodents
And we're ratting it up

Yeah, we're ratting it up
Yeah, we're ratting it up
Well, we're ratting it up
For a ratting good time tonight!

ADRIAN MITCHELL

HIS GRANGE, OR PRIVATE WEALTH

Though Clock,
To tell how night draws hence, I've none,
A Cock
I have, to sing how day draws on.
I have
A maid (my Prue) by good luck sent,
To save
That little, Fates gave me or lent.
A Hen
I keep, which creeking day by day,
Tells when
She goes her long white egg to lay.
A Goose
I have, which, with a jealous care,
Lets loose
Her tongue, to tell what danger's near.
A Lamb
I keep (tame) with my morsels fed,
Whose Dam
An Orphan left him (lately dead).
A Cat
I keep, that plays about my House
Grown fat
With eating many a miching Mouse.

Such are
But toys, to give my heart some ease:
Where care
None is, slight things do lightly please.

ROBERT HERRICK

miching = thieving

THE HEN AND THE CARP

Once, in a roostery,
there lived a speckled hen, and whenever
she laid an egg this hen
ecstatically cried:
'O progeny miraculous, particular spectaculous.
what a wonderful hen am I!'

Down in a pond nearby
perchance a gross and broody carp
was basking, but her ears were sharp –
she heard Dame Cackle cry:
'O progeny miraculous, particular spectaculous,
what a wonderful hen am I!'

'Ah, Cackle,' bubbled she,
'for your single egg, O silly one,
I lay at least a million;
suppose for each I cried:
"O progeny miraculous, particular spectaculous!"
what a hullaballoo there'd be!'

IAN SERRAILLIER

DUCKS

1.

From troubles of the world
I turn to ducks,
Beautiful comical things
Sleeping or curled
Their heads beneath white wings
By water cool,
Or finding curious things
To eat in various mucks
Beneath the pool,
Tails uppermost, or waddling
Sailor-like on the shores
Of ponds, or paddling
– Left! right! – with fanlike feet
Which are for steady oars
When they (white galleys) float
Each bird a boat
Rippling at will the sweet
Wide waterway . . .
When night is fallen *you* creep
Upstairs, but drakes and dillies
Nest with pale water-stars,
Moonbeams and shadow bars,
And water lilies;
Fearful too much to sleep
Since they've no locks

To click against the teeth
Of weasel and fox.
And warm beneath
Are eggs of cloudy green
Whence hungry rats and lean
Would stealthily suck
New life, but for the mien,
The bold ferocious mien
Of the mother-duck.

2.
Yes, ducks are valiant things
On nests of twigs and straws,
And ducks are soothy things
And lovely on the lake
When that the sunlight draws
Thereon their pictures dim
In colours cool.
And when beneath the pool
They dabble, and when they swim
And make their rippling rings,
O ducks are beautiful things!

But ducks are comical things –
As comical as you.
Quack!
They waddle round, they do.
They eat all sorts of things,
And then they quack.
By barn and stable and stack
They wander at their will,
But if you go too near
They look at you through black
Small topaz-tinted eyes
And wish you ill.

Triangular and clear
They leave their curious track
In mud at the water's edge,
And there amid the sedge
And slime they gobble and peer
Saying 'Quack! quack!'

3.

When God had finished the stars and whirl of coloured suns
He turned His mind from big things to fashion little ones,
Beautiful tiny things (like daisies) He made, and then
He made the comical ones in case the minds of men
    Should stiffen and become
    Dull, humourless and glum,
And so forgetful of their Maker be
As to take even themselves *quite seriously*.
Caterpillars and cats are lively and excellent puns:
All God's jokes are good – even the practical ones!
And as for the duck, I think God must have smiled a bit
Seeing those bright eyes blink on the day He fashioned it.
And He's probably laughing still at the sound that came out
    of its bill!

F. W. HARVEY

THE LOCH NESS MONSTER'S SONG

Sssnnnwhuffffll?
Hnwhuffl hhnnwfl hnfl hfl?
Gdroblboblhobngbl gbl gl g g g g glbgl.
Drublhaflablhaflubhafgabhaflhafl fl fl –
gm grawwwww grf grawf awfgm graw gm.
Hovoplodok – doplodovok – plovodokot-doplodokosh?
Splgraw fok fok splgrafhatchgabrlgabrl fok splfok!
Zgra kra gka fok!
Grof grawff gahf?
Gombl mbl bl –
blm plm,
blm plm,
blm plm,
blp.

EDWIN MORGAN

THE MAD GARDENER'S SONG

He thought he saw an Elephant,
    That practised on a fife:
He looked again, and found it was
    A letter from his wife.
'At length I realize,' he said,
    'The bitterness of Life!'

He thought he saw a Buffalo
    Upon the chimney-piece:
He looked again, and found it was
    His Sister's Husband's Niece.
'Unless you leave this house,' he said,
    'I'll send for the Police!'

He thought he saw a Rattlesnake
    That questioned him in Greek:
He looked again, and found it was
    The Middle of Next Week.
'The one thing I regret,' he said,
    'Is that it cannot speak!'

He thought he saw a Banker's Clerk
    Descending from the bus:
He looked again, and found it was
    A Hippopotamus.
'If this should stay to dine,' he said,
    'There won't be much for us!'

He thought he saw a Kangaroo
    That worked a coffee-mill:
He looked again, and found it was
    A Vegetable-Pill.
'Were I to swallow this,' he said,
    'I should be very ill!'

He thought he saw a Coach-and-Four
    That stood beside his bed:
He looked again, and found it was
    A Bear without a Head.
'Poor thing,' he said, 'poor silly thing!
    It's waiting to be fed!'

He thought he saw an Albatross
    That fluttered round the lamp:
He looked again, and found it was
    A Penny-Postage Stamp.
'You'd best be getting home,' he said:
    'The nights are very damp!'

He thought he saw a Garden-Door
    That opened with a key:
He looked again, and found it was
    A Double Rule of Three:
'And all its mystery,' he said,
    'Is clear as day to me!'

He thought he saw a Argument
    That proved he was the Pope:
He looked again, and found it was
    A Bar of Mottled Soap.
'A fact so dread,' he faintly said,
    'Extinguishes all hope!'

LEWIS CARROLL

CATERPILLAR

Brown and furry
Caterpillar in a hurry,
Take your walk
To the shady leaf, or stalk,
Or whatnot,
Which may be the chosen spot.
No toad spy you,
Hovering bird of prey pass by you;
Spin and die,
To live again a butterfly.

CHRISTINA ROSSETTI

SOMETHING FOR A BLUEBOTTLE

Some mother or other laid a load of white eggs
    In a rotten bit of food,
And that's how I came into the world –
    And it tasted rich and good!

We had no teeth and we had no legs,
    But we turned the stuff to soup,
And waggled and wallowed and sucked the dregs
    In our maggoty slop-group troupe!

We squirmed in our supper, we twitched in our tea
    Till we could grow no fatter,
Then we all dropped off to sleep – and that was
    The strangest part of the matter,

For we went quite hard and brown, like pods,
    And when it was time to rise,
Blow me if we hadn't been born again
    With wings this time, like – *flies*!

O I'm buzzing and blue and beautiful,
    I'm an ace at picking and stealing!
I've got masses of eyes to see you with
    And legs to run on your ceiling!

What's in the dustbin smelling so rare?
    I'm zooming in to see,
Then I'm coming to dance on your dinner – look sharp,
    You'll find no flies on me.

                                    LIBBY HOUSTON

from A MIDSUMMER NIGHT'S DREAM

You spotted snakes with double tongue,
Thorny hedgehogs, be not seen;
Newts and blindworms, do no wrong,
Come not near our fairy Queen.

Philomele, with melody
Sing in our sweet lullaby;
Lulla, lulla, lullaby, lulla, lulla, lullaby:
Never harm
Nor spell nor charm,
Come our lovely lady nigh;
So, good night, with lullaby.

Weaving spiders,come not here;
Hence, you long-legged spinners, hence!
Beetles black, approach not near;
Worm nor snail, do no offence.

Philomele, with melody
Sing in our sweet lullaby;
Lulla, lulla, lullaby, lulla, lulla, lullaby:
Never harm
Nor spell nor charm,
Come our lovely lady nigh;
So, good night, with lullaby.

WILLIAM SHAKESPEARE

IN THE BEE-FACTORY

It is night in the factory
where bees make bees,
always night and little sleep,
all the long hot summer through.

All the long dark summer through,
cradle-builders
are steadily fixing
wax to wax
for the Great Queen follows them,
stepping from rim to rim to drop
the right egg in the right cot –
she must not stop,
she cannot stop –
ten thousand cradles for making bees!

Back down the line
eggs begin hatching,
hungry grubs rising,
night-nurse bees bustling
with bee-milk to feed them,
worker-babies
to work for the factory.

Fat little grubs grow,
shed their skins,
grow again
(up the line now, new
eggs begin hatching)
till they reach the right size,
turn, and close their eyes –

Here lies the secret,
the pride of our factory!
Go to sleep maggot –
wake all bee!
Shiny legs, glossy wings,
striped backs, stings –

Success every time!
Thousands the same!
Fresh for the work ahead –
hard work till they're dead!

And what's the work?
Out in the brightness! Look,
up from the factory gate they rise
into a haze of sun and colour,
tastes to trace, sisters to tell –
their job's the sweetest
flowers to search for

to gather the pollen,
and the nectar for honey,
to feed the dark factory
where bees make bees
to fly in the brightness
gathering pollen,
and nectar for honey,
to feed the dark factory
and make
bees

LIBBY HOUSTON

12TH NOVEMBER: WINTER HONEY

To be honest, this is dark stuff; mud, tang
of bitter battery-tasting honey. The woods are in it.

Rot, decayed conglomerates, old garlic leaf, tongue wretched
by dead tastes, stubborn crystal, like rock. Ingredients:

ivy, sweat, testosterone, the blood of mites. Something human
in this flavour surely
Has all the clamber, twist and grip
of light-starved roots, and beetle borehole dust.

Deciduous flare of dead leaf,
bright lights leached out like gypsum almost, alabaster ghost.

Do not think this unkind, the effect is slow
and salty in the mouth. A body's widow in her dying year.

It is bleak with taste and like meat, gamey.

This is the offal of the flowers' nectar.
The sleep of ancient insects runs on this.

Giant's Causeway hexagons we smeared on buttered toast
or just the pellets gouged straight from wax to mouth.

Try this addiction:
compounds of starched cold, lichen-grey light. What else
    seeps out?

Much work, one bee, ten thousand flowers a day
    to make three teaspoons-worth of this
        disconcerting
        solid broth
of forest flora full of fox. Immune to wood shade now

SEAN BORODALE

PEAT CUTTING

And we left our beds in the dark
And we drove a cart to the hill
And we buried the jar of ale in the bog
And our small blades glittered in the dayspring
And we tore dark squares, thick pages
From the Book of Fire
And we spread them wet on the heather
And horseflies, poisonous hooks,
Stuck in our arms
And we laid off our coats
And our blades sank deep into water
And the lord of the bog, the kestrel,
Paced round the sun
And at noon we leaned on our tuskars
– The cold unburied jar
Touched, like a girl, a circle of burning mouths
And the boy found a wild bees' comb
And his mouth was a sudden brightness
And the kestrel fell
And a lark flashed a needle across the west
And we spread a thousand peats
Between one summer star
And the black chaos of fire at the earth's centre.

GEORGE MACKAY BROWN

THE SOUNDS OF EARTH
(*broadcast from Voyager-II to the universe*)

First, the most popular sound:
we call it talking – it's also known fondly as
shooting one's mouth off, discussing,
chewing the fat, yammering, blabbing,
conversing, confiding, debating, blabbing,
gossiping, hollering, and yakking.
So, here's a whole bunch of jaw creakers.
How come none of you guys out there
don't yap at us – we'd sure like to hear
what you have to say
on the subject of where the hell you are.

For our second selection,
we will now play a medley of music
which you may or may not care for
since as I know myself
music is a very personal thing.
Why not aim a little musical extravaganza earthward?

As I say, we're waiting.

Now for our something-for-everyone finale.
Here's a rush-hour traffic jam,
brakes are screeching – horns are blasting.
This is a phone ringing, a keyboard tapping,
and a printer whirring in the background.
I'm very partial to this next example of earth sounds:
a rocking chair creaking back and forth on a porch
accompanied by birds and crickets chirping.

To finish up, we've got a lawnmower,
knitting needles, a hammer, a saw,
a football stadium after a score,
a door shutting, a baby crying
and the ever-popular drone of television
blaring across the airways.

We're equal opportunity down here
so if you're a blob or have three heads
or look like something the cat dragged in –
we won't bat an eyelid.

JULIE O'CALLAGHAN

PLEASANT SOUNDS

The rustling of leaves under the feet in woods and under
    hedges;
The crumping of cat-ice and snow down wood-rides,
    narrow lanes, and every street causeway;
Rustling through a wood or rather rushing, while the wind
    halloos in the oak-top like thunder;
The rustle of birds' wings startled from their nests or flying
    unseen into the bushes;
The whizzing of larger birds overhead in a wood, such as
    crows, puddocks, buzzards;
The trample of robins and woodlarks on the brown leaves,
    and the patter of squirrels on the green moss;
the fall of an acorn on the ground, the pattering of nuts on
    the hazel branches as they fall from ripeness;
The flirt of the groundlark's wing from the stubbles – how
    sweet such pictures on dewy mornings, when the dew
    flashes from its brown feathers!

JOHN CLARE

BARLEY

Barley grain is like seeds of gold bullion.
When you turn a heap with a shovel it pours
With the heavy magic of wealth.
Every grain is a sleeping princess –
Her kingdom is still to come.
She sleeps with sealed lips.
Each grain is like a mouth sealed
Or an eye sealed.
In each mouth the whole bible of barley.
In each eye, the whole sun of barley.
From each single grain, given time,
You could feed the earth.

You treat them rough, dump them into the drill,
Churn them up with a winter supply
Of fertilizer, and steer out on to the tilth
Trailing your wake of grains.

When the field's finished, fresh-damp,
Its stillness is no longer stillness.
The coverlet has been drawn tight again
But now over breathing and dreams.
And water is already bustling to sponge the newcomers.
And the soil, the ancient nurse,
Is assembling everything they will need.
And the angel of earth
Is flying through the field, kissing each one awake.
But it is a hard nursery.
Night and day all through winter huddling naked
They have to listen to pitiless lessons
Of the freezing constellations
And the rain. If it were not for the sun
Who visits them daily, briefly,
To pray with them, they would lose hope
And give up. With him
They recite the Lord's prayer
And sing a psalm. And sometimes at night
When the moon haunts their field and stares down
Into their beds
They sing a psalm softly together
To keep up their courage.

Once their first leaf shivers they sing less
And start working. They cannot miss a day.
They have to get the whole thing right.
Employed by the earth, employed by the sky,
Employed by barley, to be barley.
And now they begin to show their family beauty.
They come charging over the field, under the wind, like
    warriors –
'Terrible as an army with banners',
Barbaric, tireless, Amazon battalions.

And that's how they win their kingdom.
Then they put on gold, for their coronation.
Each one barbed, feathered, a lithe weapon,
Puts on the crown of her kingdom.
Then the whole fieldful of queens
Swirls in a dance
With their invisible partner, the wind,
Like a single dancer.

That is how barley inherits the kingdom of barley.

TED HUGHES

ANSWER TO A CHILD'S QUESTION

Do you ask what the birds say? The sparrow, the dove,
The linnet and thrush say, 'I love and I love!'
In the winter they're silent – the wind is so strong;
What it says, I don't know, but it sings a loud song.
But green leaves, and blossoms, and sunny warm weather,
And singing, and loving – all come back together.
But the lark is so brimful of gladness and love,
The green fields below him, the blue sky above,
That he sings, and he sings; and forever sings he –
'I love my Love, and my Love loves me!'

SAMUEL TAYLOR COLERIDGE

HURT NO LIVING THING

Hurt no living thing,
Ladybird nor butterfly,
Nor moth with dusty wing,
Nor cricket chirping cheerily,
Nor grasshopper, so light of leap,
Nor dancing gnat,
Nor beetle fat,
Nor harmless worms that creep.

CHRISTINA ROSSETTI

RIVER

in the black gland of the earth
the tiny inkling of a river

put your ear to the river you hear trees
put your ear to the trees you hear the widening
numerical workings of the river

right down the length of Devon,
under a milky square of light that keeps quite still

the river slows down and goes on

with storm trash clustered on its branches
and paper unfolding underwater
and pairs of ducks swimming over bright grass among flooded
    willows

the earth's eye
looking through the earth's bones

carries the moon carries the sun but keeps nothing

ALICE OSWALD

THE RIVER GOD

I may be smelly and I may be old,
Rough in my pebbles, reedy in my pools,
But where my fish float by I bless their swimming
And I like the people to bathe in me, especially women.
But I can drown the fools
Who bathe too close to the weir, contrary to rules.
And they take a long time drowning
As I throw them up now and then in a spirit of clowning.
Hi yih, yippity-yap, merrily I flow,
Oh I may be an old foul river but I have plenty of go.
Once there was a lady who was too bold
She bathed in me by the tall black cliff where the water
    runs cold,
So I brought her down here
To be my beautiful dear.   →

Oh will she stay with me will she stay
This beautiful lady or will she go away?
She lies in my beautiful deep river bed with many a weed
To hold her, and many a waving reed.
Oh who would guess what a beautiful white face lies there
Waiting for me to smooth and wash away the fear
She looks at me with. Hi yih, do not let her
Go. There is no one on earth who does not forget her
Now. They say I am a foolish old smelly river
But they do not know of my wide original bed
Where the lady waits, with her golden sleepy head.
If she wishes to go I will not forgive her.

STEVIE SMITH

from GETTING TO KNOW FISH

Being a good Mohammedan, Father said:
'Friday is the day to pray and throw bread
to the fish.' In Sialkot was a river,

and I in my sailor suit four years old
walked to it holding my father's finger:
we had flour Mother had kneaded and rolled
into balls, and scraps of food grown green with mould.

From the bridge I aimed at fish, my mothballs
of flour changing shapes – first as shells
humming in the air, then like grated cheese
settling on the water as on a dish.
The fish came and swallowed, the water creased
with waves and Father said: 'Let's go pray and wish
for goodness now that we have fed the fish.'

The mosque had a goldfish pond with tiny
fish – as good a proof of God as any.
I never prayed. The Arabic was too
subtle and I'd only blow bubbles through my teeth.
I sat by the pond (a foot stuck into
the water, kicking fish when the old priest
wasn't looking) and felt heaven with my feet.

ZULFIKAR GHOSE

RAIN ON DRY GROUND

That is rain on dry ground. We heard it:
We saw the little tempest on the grass,
The panic of anticipation: heard
The uneasy leaves flutter, the air pass
In a wave, the fluster of the vegetation;

Heard the first spatter of drops, the outriders
Larruping on the road, hitting against
The gate of the drought, and shattering
On to the lances of the tottering meadow.
It is rain; it is rain on dry ground.

Rain riding suddenly out of the air,
Battering the bare walls of the sun.
It is falling on to the tongue of the blackbird,
Into the heart of the thrush; the dazed valley
Sings it down. Rain, rain on dry ground!

This is the urgent decision of the day,
The urgent drubbing of earth, the urgent raid
On the dust; downpour over the flaring poppy,
Deluge on the face of noon, the flagellant
Rain drenching across the air. The day

Flows in the ditch; bubble and twisting twig
And the sodden morning swirl along together
Under the crying hedge. And where the sun
Ran on the scythes, the rain runs down
The obliterated field, the blunted crop.

The rain stops.
The air is sprung with green.
The intercepted drops
Fall at their leisure; and between
The threading runnels on the slopes
The snail drags his caution into the sun.

CHRISTOPHER FRY

THUNDER

And suddenly the giants tired of play. –
With huge, rough hands they flung the gods' gold balls
And silver harps and mirrors at the walls
Of Heaven, and trod, ashamed, where lay
The loveliness of flowers. Frightened Day
On white feet ran from out the temple halls,
The blundering dark was filled with great war-calls,
And Beauty, shamed, slunk silently away.

Be quiet, little wind among the leaves
That turn pale faces to the coming storm.
Be quiet, little foxes in your lairs,
And birds and mice be still – a giant grieves
For his forgotten might. Hark now the warm
And heavy stumbling down the leaven stairs!

ELIZABETH BISHOP

SNOW

In the gloom of whiteness,
In the great silence of snow,
A child was sighing
And bitterly saying: 'Oh,
They have killed a white bird up there on her nest,
The down is fluttering from her breast!'
And still it fell through that dusky brightness
On the child crying for the bird of the snow.

EDWARD THOMAS

SNOW AND SNOW

Snow is sometimes a she, a soft one.
    Her kiss on your cheek, her finger on your sleeve
In early December, on a warm evening,
        And you turn to meet her, saying 'It's snowing!'
            But it is not. And nobody's there.
            Empty and calm is the air.

Sometimes the snow is a he, a sly one.
    Weakly he signs the dry stone with a damp spot.
Waifish he floats and touches the pond and is not.
        Treacherous-beggarly he falters, and taps at the window.
            A little longer he clings to the grass-blade tip
            Getting his grip.

Then how she leans, how furry foxwrap she nestles
    The sky with her warm, and the earth with her softness.
How her lit crowding fairytales sink through the space-silence
        To build her palace, till it twinkles in starlight –
            Too frail for a foot
            Or a crumb of soot.

Then how his muffled armies move in all night
    And we wake and every road is blockaded
Every hill taken and every farm occupied
    And the white glare of his tents is on the ceiling.
    And all that dull blue day and on into the
                                            gloaming
    We have to watch more coming.

Then everything in the rubbish-heaped world
    Is a bridesmaid at her miracle.
Dunghills and crumbly dark old barns are bowed in the
                                    chapel of her sparkle,
    The gruesome boggy cellars of the wood
        Are a wedding of lace
        Now taking place.

TED HUGHES

JANUARY COLD DESOLATE

January cold desolate;
February all dripping wet;
March wind ranges;
April changes;
Birds sing in tune
To flowers of May,
And sunny June
Brings longest day;
In scorched July
The storm-clouds fly
Lightning torn;
August bears corn,
September fruit;
In rough October
Earth must disrobe her;
Stars fall and shoot
In keen November;
And night is long
And cold is strong
In bleak December.

CHRISTINA ROSSETTI

AT NINE OF THE NIGHT
I OPENED MY DOOR

At nine of the night I opened my door
That stands midway between moor and moor,
And all around me, silver-bright,
I saw that the world had turned to white.

Thick was the snow on field and hedge
And vanished was the river-sedge,
Where winter skilfully had wound
A shining scarf without a sound.

And as I stood and gazed my fill
A stable boy came down the hill.
With every step I saw him take
Flew at his heel a puff of flake.

His brow was whiter than the hoar,
A beard of freshest snow he wore,
And round about him, snowflake starred,
A red horse-blanket from the yard.

In a red cloak I saw him go,
His back was bent, his step was slow,
And as he laboured through the cold
He seemed a hundred winters old.

I stood and watched the snowy head,
The whiskers white, the cloak of red.
'A Merry Christmas!' I heard him cry.
'The same to you, old friend,' said I.

CHARLES CAUSLEY

A LIGHT EXISTS IN SPRING

A Light exists in Spring
Not present on the Year
At any other period –
When March is scarcely here

A Colour stands abroad
On Solitary Fields
That Science cannot overtake
But Human Nature feels.

It waits upon the Lawn,
It shows the furthest Tree
Upon the furthest Slope you know
It almost speaks to you.

Then as Horizons step
Or Noons report away
Without the Formula of sound
It passes and we stay –

A quality of loss
Affecting our Content
As Trade had suddenly encroached
Upon a Sacrament.

EMILY DICKINSON

IN JUST-

in Just-
spring   when the world is mud-
luscious the little
lame balloonman

whistles   far   and wee

and eddieandbill come
running from marbles and
piracies and it's
spring

when the world is puddle-wonderful

the queer
old balloonman whistles
far   and   wee
and bettyandisbel come dancing

from hop-scotch and jump-rope and

it's
spring
and
     the
          goat-footed

balloonMan   whistles
far
and
wee

E. E. CUMMINGS

THE SONG OF WANDERING AENGUS

I went out to the hazel wood,
Because a fire was in my head,
And cut and peeled a hazel wand,
And hooked a berry to a thread;
And when white moths were on the wing,
And moth-like stars were flickering out,
I dropped a berry in a stream
And caught a little silver trout.

When I had laid it on the floor
I went to blow the fire aflame,
But something rustled on the floor,
And someone called me by my name:
It had become a glimmering girl
With apple blossom in her hair
Who called me by my name and ran
And faded through the brightening air.

Though I am old with wandering
Through hollow lands and hilly lands,
I will find out where she has gone,
And kiss her lips and take her hands;
And walk among long dappled grass,
And pluck till time and times are done
The silver apples of the moon,
The golden apples of the sun.

W. B. YEATS

THE LONG GARDEN

It was the garden of the golden apples,
A long garden between a railway and a road,
In the sow's rooting where the hen scratches
We dipped our fingers in the pockets of God.

In the thistly hedge old boots were flying sandals
By which we travelled through the childhood skies,
Old buckets rusty-holed with half-hung handles
Were drums to play when old men married wives.

The pole that lifted the clothes line in the middle
Was the flagpole on a prince's palace when
We looked at it through fingers crossed to riddle
In evening sunlight miracles for men.

It was the garden of the golden apples,
And when the Carrick train went by we knew
That we could never die till something happened
Like wishing for a fruit that never grew,

Or wanting to be up on Candle-Fort
Above the village with its shops and mill.
The racing cyclists' gasp-gapped reports
Hinted of pubs where life can drink his fill.

And when the sun went down into Drumcatton
And the New Moon by its little finger swung
From the telegraph wires, we knew how God had happened
And what the blackbird in the whitethorn sang.

It was the garden of the golden apples,
The halfway house where we had stopped a day
Before we took the west road to Drumcatton
Where the sun was always setting on the play.

PATRICK KAVANAGH

THE RAILWAY CHILDREN

When we climbed the slopes of the cutting
We were eye-level with the white cups
Of the telegraph poles and the sizzling wires.

Like lovely freehand they curved for miles
East and miles west beyond us, sagging
Under their burden of swallows.

We were small and thought we knew nothing
Worth knowing. We thought words travelled the wires
In the shiny pouches of raindrops,

Each one seeded full with the light
Of the sky, the gleam of the lines, and ourselves
So infinitesmally scaled

We could stream through the eye of a needle.

SEAMUS HEANEY

THE NIGHT EXPRESS

Who heard a whistle in the night, so far,
Who heard the whistle of the train pass?
– I heard,
Said a hedge-safe bird,
– And I, said the bleached grass.
– I heard, said the sinking star,
– And I, said the apple, nested on the ground,
– And I, the mooned church tower said,
– And I, the graves around.
– And you, said the roof of the farm overhead
To the child in bed,
You heard the sound.
– I, said the child, asleep almost,
I heard it plain,
I heard the whistle, the whistle of the train,
Like a friend, like a ghost.

FRANCES CORNFORD

NIGHT MAIL

This is the night mail crossing the border,
Bringing the cheque and the postal order,
Letters for the rich, letters for the poor,
The shop at the corner and the girl next door.
Pulling up Beattock, a steady climb –
The gradient's against her, but she's on time.
Past cotton grass and moorland boulder
Shovelling white steam over her shoulder,
Snorting noisily as she passes
Silent miles of wind-bent grasses.
Birds turn their heads as she approaches,
Stare from the bushes at her blank-faced coaches.
Sheepdogs cannot turn her course,
They slumber on with paws across.
In the farm she passes no one wakes,
But the jug in the bedroom gently shakes.

Dawn freshens, the climb is done.
Down towards Glasgow she descends
Towards the steam tugs yelping down the glade of cranes,
Towards the fields of apparatus, the furnaces
Set on the dark plain like gigantic chessmen.
All Scotland waits for her:
In the dark glens, beside the pale-green lochs
Men long for news.

Letters of thanks, letters from banks,
Letters of joy from girl and boy,
Receipted bills and invitations
To inspect new stock or visit relations,
And applications for situations
And timid lovers' declarations
And gossip, gossip from all the nations,
News circumstantial, news financial.
Letters with holiday snaps to enlarge in,
Letters with faces scrawled in the margin,
Letters from uncles, cousins and aunts,
Letters to Scotland from the South of France,
Letters of condolence to Highlands and Lowlands,
Notes from overseas to Hebrides –
Written on paper of every hue,
The pink, the violet, the white and the blue,
The chatty, the catty, the boring, adoring,
The cold and official and the heart's outpouring,
Clever, stupid, short and long,
The typed and the printed and the spelt all wrong.
Thousands are still asleep
Dreaming of terrifying monsters,
Of a friendly tea beside the band at Cranston's or
     Crawford's:
Asleep in working Glasgow, asleep in well-set
     Edinburgh,

Asleep in granite Aberdeen.
They continue their dreams;
But shall wake soon and long for letters,
And none will hear the postman's knock
Without a quickening of the heart,
For who can hear and feel himself forgotten?

W. H. AUDEN

GREAT-GRANDMOTHER'S LAMENT

I used to think that children loved to see their granny.
I don't know what it is. I stand at the windae.
I've never had them running intae see me.
They are no here for mair than two minutes
and then they're running away from me, bony hands,
like I'm a bad auld witch spitting oot curses.
In then oot and I'm lucky if I get a chance to press
a pound into their hand; then it's up – off – away.
Nobody says *hooray*! Nobody bothers her shirt about me.
They're that glad to see the back of me:
round shoulders, hunched old woman, sticky-oot back.
Naebody's got a minute fir their granny.
If they would jist say, 'Granny, you'll never guess what?'
it would make their old granny so happy.
But you never get to hear onything; it's all whispers.
I huv tae say, 'What's she saying?' because she
sits there, little madam, and mumbles and mutters,
and I canny understand a word, and she's moody.
My great-grandchildren get served hand and foot
and here's me still cooking for myself –
my wee bit of veg, boiled ham. Nobody bothers
staying for longer than a pound coin sucked intae a wee fist.
I'm telling you. I'm not kidding you on.
It's no like the past for grannies these days:
nobody brings their granny a wee sweetie, a hazlenut toffee,
or sips their granny's sugary tea.

Everybody is that busy behind the TV screens;
nobody knows how to make a conversation
let alone make a home-made meal or a fresh baked scone.
I'm not kidding you on. They're good for nothing.
Oh, we're the poorer for it, the hale human race.
I'll tell you, I'll be gled tae get shot o' this place.

JACKIE KAY

THE STRANGE VISITOR

A wife was sitting at her reel ae night;
And aye she sat, and aye she reeled, and aye she wished for
company.

In came a pair o' braid braid soles, and sat down at the
fireside;
And aye she sat, and aye she reeled, and aye she wished for
company.

In came a pair o' sma' sma' legs, and sat down on the braid
braid soles;
And aye she sat, and aye she reeled, and aye she wished for
company.

In came a pair o' muckle muckle knees, and sat down on the
sma' sma' legs;
And aye she sat, and aye she reeled, and aye she wished for
company.

In came a pair o' sma' sma' thees, and sat down on the
muckle muckle knees;
And aye she sat, and aye she reeled, and aye she wished for
company.

In came a pair o' muckle muckle hips, and sat down on the
sma' sma' thees;
And aye she sat, and aye she reeled, and aye she wished for
company.

In came a sma' sma' waist, and sat down on the muckle
muckle hips;
And aye she sat, and aye she reeled, and aye she wished for
company.

In came a pair o' braid braid shouthers, and sat down on the
sma' sma' waist;
And aye she sat, and aye she reeled, and aye she wished for
company.

In came a sma' sma' neck, and sat down on the braid braid
shouthers;
And aye she sat, and aye she reeled, and aye she wished for
company.

In came a great big head, and sat down on the sma' sma' neck;
And aye she sat, and aye she reeled, and aye she wished for
company.

'What way hae ye sic braid braid feet?' quo' the wife.
'Muckle ganging, muckle ganging.'
'What way hae ye sic sma' sma' legs?'
'*Aih-h-h!* – late – and *wee-e-e* moul.'
'What way hae ye sic muckle muckle knees?'
'Muckle praying, muckle praying.'
'What way hae ye sic sma' sma' thees?'
'*Aih-h-h!* – late – and *wee-e-e* moul.'
'What way hae ye sic big big hips?'
'Muckle sitting, muckle sitting.'
'What way hae ye sic a sma' sma' waist?'
'*Aih-h-h!* – late – and *wee-e-e* moul.'
'What way hae ye sic braid braid shouthers?'
'Wi' carrying broom, wi' carrying broom.'
'What way hae ye sic sma' sma' arms?'
'*Aih-h-h!* – late – and *wee-e-e* moul.'
'What way hae ye sic a muckle muckle head?'
'Muckle wit, muckle wit.'
'What do you come for?'
'For YOU!'

ANON.

GREEN CANDLES

'There's someone at the door,' said gold candlestick:
'Let her in quick, let her in quick!'
'There is a small hand groping at the handle.
'Why don't you turn it?' asked green candle.

'Don't go, don't go,' said the Hepplewhite chair,
'Lest you find a strange lady there.'
'Yes, stay where you are,' whispered the white wall:
'There is nobody there at all.'

'I know her little foot,' grey carpet said:
'Who but I should know her light tread?'
'She shall come in,' answered the open door,
'And not,' said the room, 'go out any more.'

HUMBERT WOLFE

EXPECTING VISITORS

I heard you were coming and
Thrum thrum thrum
Went something in my heart like a
Drum drum drum.

I briskly walked down the
Street street street
To buy lovely food for us to
Eat eat eat.

I cleaned the house and filled it with
Flowers flowers flowers
And asked the sun to drink up the
Showers showers showers.

Steadily purring
Thrum thrum thrum
Went the drum in my heart because
You'd come come come.

JENNY JOSEPH

A RECOLLECTION

My father's friend came once to tea.
He laughed and talked. He spoke to me.
But in another week they said
That friendly pink-faced man was dead.

'How sad . . .' they said, 'the best of men . . .'
So I said too, 'How sad'; but then
Deep in my heart I thought, with pride,
'I know a person who has died'.

FRANCES CORNFORD

THERE WAS AN OLD LADY

There was an old lady who swallowed a fly,
I don't know why she swallowed a fly,
Perhaps she'll die.

There was an old lady who swallowed a spider,
That wriggled and jiggled and tickled inside her,
She swallowed the spider to catch the fly,
I don't know why she swallowed the fly,
Perhaps she'll die.

There was an old lady who swallowed a bird,
How absurd! to swallow a bird,
She swallowed the bird to catch the spider,
That wriggled and jiggled and tickled inside her,
She swallowed the spider to catch the fly,
I don't know why she swallowed the fly,
Perhaps she'll die.

There was an old lady who swallowed a cat,
Imagine that! to swallow a cat,
She swallowed the cat to catch the bird,
She swallowed the bird to catch the spider,
That wriggled and jiggled and tickled inside her,
She swallowed the spider to catch the fly,
I don't know why she swallowed the fly,
Perhaps she'll die.

There was an old lady who swallowed a dog,
What a hog! to swallow a dog,
She swallowed the dog to catch the cat,
She swallowed the cat to catch the bird,
She swallowed the bird to catch the spider,
That wriggled and jiggled and tickled inside her,
She swallowed the spider to catch the fly,
I don't know why she swallowed the fly,
Perhaps she'll die.

There was an old lady who swallowed a goat,
Just opened her throat! to swallow a goat,
She swallowed the goat to catch the dog,
She swallowed the dog to catch the cat,
She swallowed the cat to catch the bird,
She swallowed the bird to catch the spider,
That wriggled and jiggled and tickled inside her,
She swallowed the spider to catch the fly,
I don't know why she swallowed the fly,
Perhaps she'll die.

There was an old lady who swallowed a cow,
I don't know how she swallowed a cow!
She swallowed the cow to catch the goat,
She swallowed the goat to catch the dog,
She swallowed the dog to catch the cat,
She swallowed the cat to catch the bird,
She swallowed the bird to catch the spider,
That wriggled and jiggled and tickled inside her,
She swallowed the spider to catch the fly,
I don't know why she swallowed the fly,
Perhaps she'll die.

There was an old lady who swallowed a horse,
She's dead – of course!

ANON.

THE MISSING BOY
(*for Etan Patz*)

Every time we take the bus
my son sees the picture of the missing boy.
He looks at it like a mirror – the dark
straw hair, the pale skin,
the blue eyes, the electric-blue sneakers with
slashes of jagged gold. But of course that
kid is little, only six and a half,
an age when things can happen to you,
when you're not really safe, and our son is seven,
practically fully grown – why, he would
tower over that kid if they could
find him and bring him right here on this bus and
stand them together. He holds to the pole,
wishing for that, the tape on the poster
gleaming over his head, beginning to
melt at the centre and curl at the edges as it
ages. At night, when I put him to bed,
my son holds my hand tight
and says he's sure that kid's all right,
nothing to worry about, he just
hopes he's getting the food he likes,
not just any old food, but the food
he likes the most, the food he is used to.

SHARON OLDS

GRAVE BY A HOLM-OAK

You lie there, Anna,
In your grave now,
Under a snow-sky,
You lie there now.

Where have the dead gone?
Where do they live now?
Not in the grave, they say,
Then where now?

Tell me, tell me,
Is it where I may go?
Ask not, cries the holm-oak.
Weep, says the snow.

STEVIE SMITH

DEATH IS SMALLER THAN I THOUGHT

My mother and father died some years ago
I loved them very much.
When they died my love for them
Did not vanish or fade away.
It stayed just about the same,
Only a sadder colour.
And I can feel their love for me,
Same as it ever was.

Nowadays, in good times or bad,
I sometimes ask my mother and father
To walk beside me or to sit with me
So we can talk together
Or be silent.

They always come to me.
I talk to them and listen to them
And think I hear them talk to me.
It's very simple –
Nothing to do with spiritualism
Or religion or mumbo-jumbo.

It is imaginary.
It is real.
It is love.

ADRIAN MITCHELL

WHEN GOD LETS MY BODY BE

when god lets my body be

from each brave eye shall sprout a tree
fruit that dangles therefrom

the purpled world will dance upon
between my lips which did sing

a rose shall beget the spring
that maidens whom passion wastes

will lay between their little breasts
my strong fingers beneath the snow

into strenuous birds shall go
my love walking in the grass

their wings will touch with her face
and all the while shall my heart be
with the bulge and nuzzle of the sea

E. E. CUMMINGS

THE CHILD'S STORY

When I was small and they talked about love I laughed
But I ran away and I hid in a tall tree
Or I lay in asparagus beds
But I still listened.
The blue dome sang with the wildest birds
And the new sun sang in the idle noon

But then I heard love, love, sung from the steeples, each belfry,
And I was afraid and I watched the cypress trees
Join the deciduous chestnuts and oaks in a crowd of shadows
And then I shivered and ran and ran to the tall
White house with the green shutters and dark red door
And I cried 'Let me in even if you must love me'
And they came and lifted me up and told me the name
Of the near and the far stars,
And so my first love was.

ELIZABETH JENNINGS

BALLOONS

Since Christmas they have lived with us,
Guileless and clear,
Oval soul-animals,
Taking up half the space,
Moving and rubbing on the silk

Invisible air drifts,
Giving a shriek and pop
When attacked, then scooting to rest, barely trembling.
Yellow cathead, blue fish –
Such queer moons we live with

Instead of dead furniture!
Straw mats, white walls
And these travelling
Globes of thin air, red, green,
Delighting

The heart like wishes or free
Peacocks blessing
Old ground with a feather
Beaten in starry metals.
Your small

Brother is making
His balloon squeak like a cat.
Seeming to see
A funny pink world he might eat on the other side of it,
He bites,

Then sits
Back, fat jug
Contemplating a world clear as water.
A red
Shred in his little fist.

SYLVIA PLATH

WHAT ARE HEAVY?

What are heavy? Sea-sand and sorrow;
What are brief? Today and tomorrow;
What are frail? Spring blossoms and youth;
What are deep? The ocean and truth.

CHRISTINA ROSSETTI

FAIRGROUND
(*in Memory of My Father*)

There it was, Big Dipper, Giant Racer, Figure of Eight,
Any name, a fairground near the sea
And I was five years old jumping and shouting and begging you
    to take me
High up there into the clouds and the sun. You paused at first
And then went up to test the ride without me. I watched you go
Out of my sight, heard the engine pounding, saw the steep
Climb and the dips and I was all excitement, elation and when
    you came
Out of the glory of golden air you picked me up,
Put me between your knees and slowly we climbed
Up the sheerest slope I'd ever seen or felt
And I was afraid but joyfully so, you held me tight
Between your knees, your hands over mine and how could I
    know
This was the closest we'd ever be, that never again
Would there be a ride to the Heavens, you bearing me up
And me all trust and delight? The engine dipped
Down and up and down again with the élan of speed and the air
Ran through our hair, time was somewhere else
Until we began to slow and came down at last
To the usual world of flatness but I was still
Up with the sun and you holding me tight
In a closeness so sweet, in a timeless pleasure of height.

ELIZABETH JENNINGS

WHY DO YOU STAY UP SO LATE?
(*for Russ*)

I'll tell you, if you really want to know:
remember that day you lost two years ago
at the rockpool where you sat and played the jeweller
with all those stones you'd stolen from the shore?
Most of them went dark and nothing more,
but sometimes one would blink the secret colour
it had locked up somewhere in its stony sleep.
This is how you knew the ones to keep.

So I collect the dull things of the day
in which I see some possibility
but which are dead and which have the surprise
I don't know, and I've no pool to help me tell –
so I look at them and look at them until
one thing makes a mirror in my eyes
then I paint it with the tear to make it bright.
This is why I sit up through the night.

DON PATERSON

OUT IN THE DESERT

Out in the desert lies the sphinx
It never eats and it never drinx
Its body quite solid without any chinx
And when the sky's all purples and pinx
(As if it was painted with coloured inx)
And the sun it ever so swiftly sinx
Behind the hills in a couple of twinx
You may hear (if you're lucky) a bell that clinx
And also tolls and also tinx
And they say at the very same sound the sphinx
It sometimes smiles and it sometimes winx:
But nobody knows just what it thinx.

CHARLES CAUSLEY

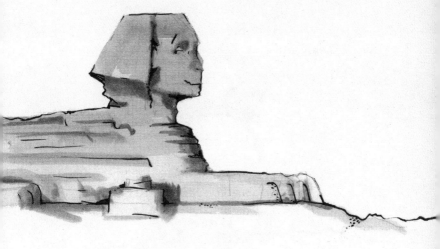

YOU ARE OLD, FATHER WILLIAM

'You are old, father William,' the young man said,
'And your hair has become very white;
And yet you incessantly stand on your head –
Do you think, at your age, it is right?'

'In my youth,' father William replied to his son,
'I feared it would injure the brain;
But now that I'm perfectly sure I have none,
Why, I do it again and again.'

'You are old,' said the youth, 'as I mentioned before,
And have grown most uncommonly fat;
Yet you turned a back-somersault in at the door –
Pray, what is the reason of that?'

'In my youth,' said the sage, as he shook his grey locks,
'I kept all my limbs very supple
By the use of this ointment – one shilling the box –
Allow me to sell you a couple.'

'You are old,' said the youth, 'and your jaws are too weak
For anything tougher than suet;
Yet you finished the goose, with the bones and the beak –
Pray, how did you manage to do it?'

'In my youth,' said his father, 'I took to the law,
And argued each case with my wife;
And the muscular strength, which it gave to my jaw,
Has lasted the rest of my life.'

'You are old,' said the youth; 'one would hardly suppose
That your eye was as steady as ever;
Yet you balanced an eel on the end of your nose –
What made you so awfully clever?'

'I have answered three questions, and that is enough,'
Said his father; 'don't give yourself airs!
Do you think I can listen all day to such stuff?
Be off, or I'll kick you down stairs!'

LEWIS CARROLL

OVERHEARD ON A SALTMARSH

Nymph, nymph, what are your beads?

Green glass, goblin. Why do you stare at them?

Give them me.

           No.

Give them me. Give them me.

                    No.

Then I will howl all night in the reeds,
Lie in the mud and howl for them.

Goblin, why do you love them so?

They are better than stars or water,
Better than voices of winds that sing,
Better than any man's fair daughter,
Your green glass beads on a silver ring.

Hush, I stole them out of the moon.

Give me your beads, I want them.

                                        No.

I will howl in a deep lagoon
For your green glass beads. I love them so.
Give them me. Give them.

                          No.

                    HAROLD MONRO

THE GOOD FRIEND OF MELANIE MOON

For the first year of my friendship with Melanie Moon
I gave her a cotton worm.
In the second year I gave her a paper spoon.
For the third, a leather piano.
For the fourth, a rose.
In the fifth year of my friendship with Melanie Moon
I gave her a wooden glove.
Year six, an iron hanky.
Year seven, a woollen book.
Year eight, a bronze banana.
Year nine, a copper hat.
In the tenth year of my friendship with Melanie Moon
I gave her a tin cat.

In year eleven I gave her slippers of steel.
In year twelve I gave her a silk cheroot.
A lace knife in thirteen.
In fourteen, an ivory wasp.
In the fifteenth year of my friendship with Melanie Moon
I gave her a crystal moth.

Melanie Moon – in our twentieth year
I gave her a china car.

Melanie Moon – in our twenty-fifth year
I gave her a silver tent.
In the thirtieth year, a pearl pear.
In year thirty-five, a coral cake.
In the fortieth year, a ruby boot.
In year forty-five, a sapphire goat.

Melanie, Melanie, Melanie Moon,
in our fiftieth year a golden umbrella.
Melanie, Melanie, Melanie Moon,
in our fifty-fifth year an emerald gun.
In the sixtieth year of our friendship
I gave her a diamond balloon
and then my friendship with Melanie Moon
was over and done.

                                    CAROL ANN DUFFY

DOUBLE TROUBLE

We were rich and poor.
We were bought and sold.

We were black and white.
We were young and old.

We were life and death.
We were north and south.

We were hand in hand.
We were foot and mouth.

We were good and bad.
We were war and peace.

We were day and night.
We were man and beast.

We were hunger and greed.
We were water and land.

We were empty and full.
We were lost and found.

We had two strings to our bow.
We were in it together.

We were the spitting image.
We were the doppelganger.

We were terrible twins.
We were happy and sad.

We were alter ego.
We were sane and mad.

We were two-faced.
We were two-a-penny.

We spat, 'Double or quits.'
We sneered, 'Double the money.'

We liked to two-time.
We stayed in a twin-town.

We led a double life.
We lived in a two-up-two-down.

We were too much.
We were entwined.

We were a right pair.
We were in two minds.

We peered through bifocals.
We talked in double entendres.

We walked double-quick.
We never wandered.

We were a double act.
We were Morecambe and Wise.

We were Laurel and Hardy.
We were Jekyll and Hyde.

We were Romeo and Juliet.
We were tragedy and comedy.

We spoke tête-à-tête.
We were a carbon copy.

We dreamed in a double bed.
We were fluently bilingual.

We were in two minds.
We were never single.

We drove on dual carriageways.
We insisted on equal pay.

We were twinned; we were mated.
We loved and we hated.

We could not be separated.
We could not be separated.

JACKIE KAY

I'M NOBODY! WHO ARE YOU?

I'm nobody! Who are you?
Are you nobody, too?
Then there's a pair of us – don't tell!
They'd banish us, you know.

How dreary to be somebody!
How public, like a frog
To tell your name the livelong day
To an admiring bog!

EMILY DICKINSON

LOVE WITHOUT HOPE

Love without hope, as when the young bird-catcher
Swept off his tall hat to the Squire's own daughter,
So let the imprisoned larks escape and fly
Singing about her head, as she rode by.

ROBERT GRAVES

MAGGIE AND MILLY AND MOLLY AND MAY

maggie and milly and molly and may
went down to the beach(to play one day)

and maggie discovered a shell that sang
so sweetly she couldn't remember her troubles,and

milly befriended a stranded star
whose rays five languid fingers were;

and molly was chased by a horrible thing
which raced sideways while blowing bubbles:and

may came home with a smooth round stone
as small as a world and as large as alone.

For whatever we lose(like a you or a me)
it's always ourselves we find in the sea.

E. E. CUMMINGS

from UNDER MILK WOOD

Johnnie Crack and Flossie Snail Kept their baby in a milking
pail Flossie Snail and Johnnie Crack One would pull it out
and one would put it back

O it's my turn now said Flossie Snail To take the baby from
the milking pail And it's my turn now said Johnnie Crack To
smack it on the head and put it back

Johnnie Crack and Flossie Snail Kept their baby in a milking
pail One would put it back and one would pull it out And
all it had to drink was ale and stout For Johnnie Crack and
Flossie Snail Always used to say that stout and ale Was good
for a baby in a milking pail.

DYLAN THOMAS

THE NOSE
(*after* Gogol)

The nose went away by itself
in the early morning
while its owner was asleep.
It walked along the road
sniffing at everything.

It thought: I have a personality of my own.
Why should I be attached to a body?
I haven't been allowed to flower.
So much of me has been wasted.

And it felt wholly free.
It almost began to dance
The world was so full of scents
it had had no time to notice,

when it was attached to a face
weeping, being blown,
catching all sorts of germs
and changing colour.

But now it was quite at ease
bowling merrily along
like a hoop of a wheel,
a factory packed with scent.

And all would have been well
but that, round about evening,
having no eyes for guides,
it staggered into the path
of a mouth, and it was gobbled
rapidly like a sausage
and chewed by great sour teeth –
and that was how it died.

IAIN CRICHTON SMITH

THERE WAS A NAUGHTY BOY

There was a naughty Boy,
And a naughty Boy was he,
He ran away to Scotland
The people for to see –

Then he found
That the ground
Was as hard,
That a yard
Was as long,
That a song
Was as merry,
That a cherry
Was as red –
That lead
Was as weighty,
That fourscore
Was as eighty,
That a door
Was as wooden
As in England –

So he stood in his shoes
And he wonder'd,
He wonder'd,
He stood in his shoes
And he wonder'd.

JOHN KEATS

WHAT IS PINK?

What is pink? A rose is pink
By the fountain's brink.
What is red? A poppy's red
In its barley bed.
What is blue? The sky is blue
Where the clouds float through.
What is white? A swan is white
Sailing in the light.
What is yellow? Pears are yellow,
Rich and ripe and mellow.
What is green? The grass is green,
With small flowers between.
What is violet? Clouds are violet
In the summer twilight.
What is orange? Why, an orange,
Just an orange!

CHRISTINA ROSSETTI

THE AKOND OF SWAT

Who or why, or which, or *what*,

                     Is the Akond of SWAT?

Is he tall or short, or dark or fair?
Does he sit on a stool or a sofa or chair, or SQUAT,

                     The Akond of Swat?

Is he wise or foolish, young or old?
Does he drink his soup and his coffee cold, or HOT,

                     The Akond of Swat?

Does he sing or whistle, jabber or talk,
And when riding abroad does he gallop or walk, or TROT,

                     The Akond of Swat?

Does he wear a turban, a fez, or a hat?
Does he sleep on a mattress, a bed, or a mat, or a COT,
                The Akond of Swat?

When he writes a copy in round-hand size,
Does he cross his T's and finish his I's with a DOT,
                The Akond of Swat?

Can he write a letter concisely clear
Without a speck or a smudge or smear or BLOT,
                The Akond of Swat?

Do his people like him extremely well?
Or do they, whenever they can, rebel, or PLOT,
                At the Akond of Swat?

If he catches them then, either old or young,
Does he have them chopped in pieces or hung, or SHOT,
                The Akond of Swat?

Do his people prig in the lanes or park?
Or even at times, when days are dark, GAROTTE?
                              O the Akond of Swat!

Does he study the wants of his own dominion?
Or doesn't he care for public opinion a JOT,
                              The Akond of Swat?

To amuse his mind do his people show him
Pictures, or anyone's last new poem, or WHAT,
                              For the Akond of Swat?

At night if he suddenly screams and wakes,
Do they bring him only a few small cakes, or a LOT,
                              For the Akond of Swat?

Does he live on turnips, tea or tripe?
Does he like his shawl to be marked with a stripe, or a DOT,
                              The Akond of Swat?

Does he like to lie on his back in a boat
Like the lady who lived in that isle remote, SHALLOTT,
                              The Akond of Swat?

Is he quiet, or always making a fuss?
Is his steward a Swiss or a Swede or a Russ, or a SCOT,
                              The Akond of Swat?

Does he like to sit by the calm blue wave?
Or to sleep and snore in a dark green cave, or a GROTT,
            The Akond of Swat?

Does he drink small beer from a silver jug?
Or a bowl? or a glass? or a cup? or a mug? or a POT,
            The Akond of Swat?

Does he beat his wife with a gold-topped pipe,
When she lets the gooseberries grow too ripe, or ROT,
            The Akond of Swat?

Does he wear a white tie when he dines with friends,
And tie it neat in a bow with ends, or a KNOT,
            The Akond of Swat?

Does he like new cream, and hate mince pies?
When he looks at the sun does he wink his eyes, or NOT,
The Akond of Swat?

Does he teach his subjects to roast and bake?
Does he sail about on an inland lake, in a YACHT,
The Akond of Swat?

Someone, or nobody, knows I wot
Who or which or why or what
Is the Akond of Swat!

EDWARD LEAR

LAUGHTER IS AN EGG

Laughter is an egg
that does a one-leg hop
Laughter is an egg
that can outspin a top

Laughter is an egg
with a crick-crack face
that can hide in the heart
of the human race.

JOHN AGARD

BED IN SUMMER

In Winter I get up at night
And dress by yellow candlelight.
In Summer, quite the other way,
I have to go to bed by day.

I have to go to bed and see
The birds still hopping on the tree,
Or hear the grown-up people's feet
Still going past me in the street.

And does it not seem hard to you,
When all the sky is clear and blue,
And I should like so much to play,
To have to go to bed by day?

ROBERT LOUIS STEVENSON

JABBERWOCKY

'Twas brillig, and the slithy toves
Did gyre and gimble in the wabe;
All mimsy were the borogoves,
And the mome raths outgrabe.

'Beware the Jabberwock, my son!
The jaws that bite, the claws that catch!
Beware the Jubjub bird, and shun
The frumious Bandersnatch!'

He took his vorpal sword in hand:
Long time the manxome foe he sought –
So rested he by the Tumtum tree,
And stood a while in thought.

And, as in uffish thought he stood,
The Jabberwock, with eyes of flame,
Came whiffling through the tulgey wood,
And burbled as it came!

One two! One two! And through and through
The vorpal blade went snicker-snack!
He left it dead, and with its head
He went galumphing back.

'And hast thou slain the Jabberwock?
Come to my arms, my beamish boy!
Oh frabjous day! Callooh! Callay!'
He chortled in his joy.

'Twas brillig, and the slithy toves
Did gyre and gimble in the wabe;
All mimsy were the borogoves,
And the mome raths outgrabe.

LEWIS CARROLL

EPILOGUE

I have crossed an ocean
I have lost my tongue
from the root of the old one
a new one has sprung.

GRACE NICHOLS

THE MOON AT KNOWLE HILL

The moon was married last night
and nobody saw
dressed up in her ghostly dress
for the summer ball.

The stars shimmied in the sky
and danced a whirligig;
the moon vowed to be true
and lit up the corn-rigs.

She kissed the dark lips of the sky
Above the summer house
She in her pale white dress
swooned across the vast sky

The moon was married last night
the beautiful belle of the ball
and nobody saw her at all
except a small girl in a navy dress

who witnessed it all.

JACKIE KAY

A STAR HERE AND A STAR THERE

the first whisper of stars is a faint thing
a candle sound, too far away to read by

the first whisper of stars is a candle sound
those faraway stars that rise and give themselves airs
    a star here and a star there
the first whisper of stars is that faint thing
that candle sound too far away to read by

when you walk outside leaving the door ajar
and smell the various Danks of Dusk
    and a star here
    and a star there

you walk outside leaving the door ajar
and one by one those stars bring you their troubles and a star
those deafmute stars – Alkaid Mizar Alioth—
trying to make you hear who they once were
    and a star
    here and there
    and
    here and there the
    start of a
Phad Merak Muscida – it's like blowing on a ring of cinders
all that sky that lies hidden in the taken for granted air

it's like blowing on a ring of cinders
the crackle of not quite stars that you can hear
when you walk outside leaving the door ajar
and smell the various Danks of Dusk
and here and there
the start
of a star

someone looks up, he sees his soul growing visible
in various shapes above the house

he sees his soul tilted above the house
all his opponent selves hanging and fluttering
out there in the taken for granted air
in various shapes above the house
    star
he sees a star here and a star there
and a star here
and a star a star
here and there he sees

there flies that man they call the moon,
that bone-thin man, his body almost gone
    star
there he flies among the stars,
that deafmute man, urgently making signs
among those first faint stars
those whispered stars, their meanings almost gone

ALICE OSWALD

ADULT FICTION

I always loved libraries, the quiet of them,
The smell of the plastic covers and the paper
And the tables and the silence of them,
The silence of them that if you listened wasn't silence,
It was the murmur of stories held for years on shelves
And the soft clicking of the date stamp,
The soft clickety-clicking of the date stamp.

I used to go down to our little library on a Friday night
In late summer, just as autumn was thinking about
Turning up, and the light outside would be the colour
Of an Everyman cover and the lights in the library
Would be soft as anything, and I'd sit at a table
And flick through a book and fall in love
With the turning of the leaves, the turning of the leaves.

And then at seven o'clock Mrs Dove would say
In a voice that wasn't too loud so it wouldn't
Disturb the books 'Seven o'clock please . . .'
And as I was the only one in the library's late summer rooms
I would be the only one to stand up and close my book
And put it back on the shelf with a sound like a kiss,
Back on the shelf with a sound like a kiss.

And I'd go out of the library and Mrs Dove would stand
For a moment silhouetted by the Adult Fiction,
And then she would turn the light off and lock the door
And go to her little car and drive off into the night
That was slowly turning the colour of ink and I would stand
For two minutes and then I'd walk over to the dark library
And just stand in front of the dark library.

IAN McMILLAN

INDEX OF FIRST LINES

INDEX OF POETS

ACKNOWLEDGEMENTS

The compiler and publisher wish to thank the following for permission to use copyright material:

Agard, John, 'Laughter is an Egg', by permission of Caroline Sheldon Literary Agency on behalf of the author; **Auden, W. H**, 'Night Mail', by permission of Curtis Brown Ltd on behalf of the author; **Borodale, Sean**, '12th November: Winter Honey', from *The Bee Journal*, by permission of the author c/o Rogers, Coleridge & White Ltd; **Causley, Charles**, 'Good Morning, Mr Croco-doco-dile', 'At Nine of the Night I Opened My Door' and 'Out in the Desert', by permission of David Higham Associates Ltd on behalf of the author; **Clarke, Gillian**, 'First Words' and 'The Fox and the Girl', from *Recipe for Water*, by permission of Carcanet Press; **Cornford, Frances**, 'The Night Express' and 'A Recollection', from *Selected Poems*, by permission of Enitharmon Press; **Crichton Smith, Iain**, 'The Nose', from *Collected Poems*, by permission of Carcanet Press; **cummings, e. e**, 'in Just-', copyright 1923, 1951, © 1991, by the Trustees for the e. e. cummings Trust, copyright © 1976 by George James Firmage, 'when god lets my body be', copyright 1923, 1951, © 1991, by the Trustees for the e. e. cummings Trust, copyright © 1976 by George James Firmage, from *Complete Poems: 1904–1962*, edited by George J. Firmage, by permission of Liveright Publishing Corporation, 'maggie and milly and molly and may', copyright © 1956, 1984, 1991 by the Trustees for the e. e. cummings Trust; **Dharker, Imtiaz**, 'How to Cut a Pomegranate', from *The Terrorist at My Table* (2006), by permission of Bloodaxe Books; **Duffy, Carol Ann**, 'F for Fox', 'A Crow and a Scarecrow' and 'The Good Friend of Melanie Moon', by permission of

the author; **Edgar, Marriott**, 'The Lion and Albert', words
and music by George Marriott Edgar (1933), reproduced by
permission of EMI Music Publishing Limited; **Graves, Robert**,
'Love without Hope', from *Complete Poems in One Volume*,
by permission of Carcanet Press; **Harvey, F. W.**, 'Ducks', from
Ducks and Other Verses, by permission of Eileen Griffiths (née
Harvey); **Heaney, Seamus**, 'St Francis and the Birds', from
Death of a Naturalist, 'The Railway Children', from *Opened
Ground*, reprinted by permission of Faber and Faber Ltd;
Hegley, John, 'The Emergensea', from *My Dog Is A Carrot*,
Walker Books (2002), by permission of United Agents
on behalf of the author; **Houston, Libby**, 'The Dragonfly',
'The Dream of the Cabbage Caterpillars', 'Something for
a Bluebottle' and 'In the Bee-Factory', from *All Change*,
OUP, by permission of the author; **Hughes, Ted**, 'Horrible
Song', 'Rat-Psalm', 'Barley' and 'Snow and Snow', reprinted
by permission of Faber and Faber Ltd; **Jennings, Elizabeth**,
'The Sleep of Birds', 'The Child's Story' and 'Fairground',
from *Collected Poems*, Carcanet Press, by permission of David
Higham Associates Ltd on behalf of the author; **Joseph,
Jenny**, 'Expecting Visitors', by permission of Johnson and
Alcock on behalf of the author; **Kavanagh, Patrick**, 'The
Long Garden', by kind permission of the Trustees of the Estate
of the late Katherine B. Kavanagh, through the Jonathan
Williams Literary Agency; **Kay, Jackie**, 'Great-Grandmother's
Lament', 'Double Trouble' and 'The Moon at Knowle Hill',
from *Red Cherry Red* (2007), by permission of Bloomsbury
Publishing Plc; **Kinnell, Galway**, 'Blackberry Eating', from
Selected Poems (2001), by permission of Bloodaxe Books;
MacCaig, Norman, 'Caterpillar' and 'Toad', by permission
of Berlinn Limited; **McMillan, Ian**, 'Ten Things Found
in a Shipwrecked Sailor's Pocket' and 'Adult Fiction', by

permission of UK Touring on behalf of the author; **Mitchell, Adrian**, 'Stufferation', 'Rat It Up' and 'Death Is Smaller Than I Thought', from *Come On Everybody: Poems 1953–2008* (2012), by permission of Bloodaxe Books; **Morgan, Edwin**, 'The Apple's Song', 'Hyena' and 'The Loch Ness Monster's Song', from *Collected Poems* (1988), by permission of Carcanet Press; **Nichols, Grace**, 'Epilogue', from *I Is a Long Memoried Woman*, by permission of Karnak House; **O'Callaghan, Julie**, 'The Sounds of Earth', from *Tell Me This Is Normal*, Bloodaxe Books (2008), by permission of the author; **Olds, Sharon**, 'The Missing Boy', by permission of The Random House Group UK; **Oswald, Alice**, 'River' and 'A Star Here and a Star There', reprinted by permission of Faber and Faber Ltd; **Paterson, Don**, 'Why Do You Stay Up So Late', from *Selected Poems*, by permission of the author c/o Rogers, Coleridge & White Ltd; **Plath, Sylvia**, 'Balloons', from *Selected Poems*, reprinted by permission of Faber and Faber Ltd; **Serraillier, Ian**, 'The Hen and the Carp', first published in *Thomas and the Sparrow*, Oxford University Press (1946), by permission of the Estate of Ian Serraillier; **Smith, Stevie**, 'The Forlorn Sea', 'The River God' and 'Grave by a Holm-Oak', by permission of the estate of James MacGibbon; **Sweeney, Matthew**, 'Fishbones Dreaming', reprinted by permission of Faber and Faber Ltd; **Thomas, Dylan**, 'Johnnie Crack and Flossie Snail', extract from *Under Milk Wood*, by permission of David Higham Associates Ltd on behalf of the author; **Williams, William Carlos**, 'This Is Just to Say', from *Collected Poems Volume 1*, by permission of Carcanet Press.

Every effort has been made to trace the copyright holders, but if any have been inadvertently overlooked the publisher will be pleased to make the necessary arrangement at the first opportunity.

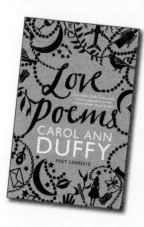

Also by
CAROL ANN DUFFY
published by Macmillan

Also by
EMILY GRAVETT
published by Macmillan

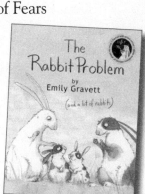

Again!
Matilda's Cat
Wolf Won't Bite!
Dogs
Blue Chameleon
The Odd Egg
The Rabbit Problem
Cave Baby
Monkey and Me
Spells
Orange Pear Apple Bear
Little Mouse's Big Book of Fears
Meerkat Mail
Wolves